W9-CFT-018

Movers, Dreamers, and Risk-Takers

MOVERS
DREAMERS
and Risk-Takers

UNLOCKING THE POWER OF ADHD

Kevin Roberts

HAZELDEN®

Hazelden
Center City, Minnesota 55012
hazelden.org

© 2012 by Kevin J. Roberts
All rights reserved. Published 2012
Printed in the United States of America

No part of this publication may be reproduced, stored in a retrieval system, or trans-
mitted in any form or by any means—electronic, mechanical, photocopying, recording,
scanning, or otherwise—without the express written permission of the publisher.
Failure to comply with these terms may expose you to legal action and damages for
copyright infringement.

Library of Congress Cataloging-in-Publication Data
Roberts, Kevin J.
    Movers, dreamers, and risk-takers : unlocking the power of ADHD /
Kevin Roberts.—1st ed.
        p. cm.
    Includes bibliographical references.
    ISBN 978-1-61649-204-5 (softcover)
    1. Roberts, Kevin J. 2. Attention-deficit hyperactivity disorder—Diagnosis—
Humor. 3. Attention-deficit-disordered children—Biography. 4. Attention-deficit-
disordered adults—Biography. 5. Male comedians—Biography. I. Title.
RJ506.H9R627 2012
618.92'85890092 — dc23
[B]
                                                                2012001950

Editor's notes

The names, details, and circumstances may have been changed to protect the privacy
of those mentioned in this publication.

This publication is not intended as a substitute for the advice of health care professionals.

The lyrics on page 163 are from *The Bible Beat* written by Fr. E. N. Donoher, C.S.B.,
© 1976.

16 15 14 13 12   1 2 3 4 5 6

Cover design by Theresa Gedig
Interior design and typesetting by Percolator

To the Boys and Girls Clubs of America.
You helped father a fatherless boy.

CONTENTS

ACKNOWLEDGMENTS

I am blessed with many friends and family members who supported me in writing this book:

- My mother, for blessing and encouraging my authentic nature.

- Arthur Robin, for providing me and the world with a font of wisdom, compassion, and tireless service to others.

- Tom and Ann Houston, for their ongoing support of my development as a writer.

- Alex Puzey, for forcing me to practice what I preach.

- Ryan Fitzpatrick, for showing me the power of personal transformation in action.

- Weenie Woo, for allowing me to participate in a process that has culminated in her becoming a very fine person.

- The Roeper School, for helping me grow up.

- Nancy Webster and Mike Ruddy, for believing in me.

- Garrett Reeves and Asa Watten, for teaching me the wisdom of Zellstein.

- John Everingham, for being a powerful mentor these last sixteen years.

- My family, for blessing me on my journey and always encouraging me, and for allowing me to use their stories.

- Tony Vicich, for inspiring me to reach for my dreams, and for showing me how to view comedy as an art form.

- Alex Hogan, for steadfastness and equilibrium in an environment that can be chaotic.

- The parents of my ADHD students and clients, for trusting me with their most precious commodity.

- David Wolfe, for convincing me that I was a writer, and for challenging much of my toxic shame.

- Dilly Dally, for consistently being willing to support me.

- Fran and Phil Parker, for great food, connection, camaraderie, and joy.

- Susanne Fest, for supporting and encouraging me through the detail-oriented process of my master's degree.

- Antioch University, for empowering me to learn what I wanted to learn.

- Jack Wagner and Logan Wiand, for showing me that intelligence comes in many different packages.

- Blair and her sister Madison, for being de facto publicists for my work.

- Chris Caretti, for much-appreciated humor.

- Doug Rutley, for accepting all of me without condition.

- Nahr Hing, for filling in the pregnant pauses of life with meaning and sustenance.

- CHADD, for making me feel at home.

- Terry Matlen, for sending a lot of people my way in my early years of practice.

- Nick Berry, for modeling perseverance for me.

- Liana Roberts, for being my Cheerleader-in-Chief.

- The extended Colman families, for supporting me by sending new clients my way, and for allowing me to help when needed.

- Geri Markel, for just being authentic.

- Dan Campion, for always looking out for me and doing the chores for my mother that I am often too busy, or too lazy, to do.

- David Knight, for providing me with unique stories that I regularly use to entertain.

- Alejandro Sanchez, for too many things to list.

- Barb Evangelista, for simply being "Barba-ji."

- The Stavoes, Nagles, Harneds, LaHautes, and Kelly, for being patient and caring neighbors.

- Palmer Stevens, for supporting me in numerous and various ways.

- Ross Willard, Adam Seyburn, and the "Brainiac2," for helping me handle the details of school with our students so that I get to spend more time being the goofy guy that I really am.

- Tim Kowalski, for showing me how to serve others.

- Lambrini, Alex, Angie, Christos, and the folks at Monty's Grill, for providing me with inspiration, support, and a place to write these many years.

- All the folks I have worked with professionally, for trusting me with their stories.

- Janet Thompson, for letting me use her Sears self-correcting electric typewriter in high school.

- Dr. Joel Glieberman, for helping me overcome a lot of my anxiety.

- Dylan Shallow, for making my work fun!

- Paul Soczynski, for seeing my gold when I could not.

- Danny Coleman, Thomas Martins, Danny Parks, Ray Campise, Hayden Hickory, and all the "Troy Boys" who enlivened my work.

INTRODUCTION

*"The pessimist sees difficulty in every opportunity.
The optimist sees the opportunity in every difficulty."*
Winston Churchill

I am a stand-up comedian. I have performed all over the country at comedy clubs, conferences, and conventions. I make people laugh, and in my daily life I keep those around me entertained. I've been doing this since I was a small boy. And I owe these abilities to ADHD (attention-deficit/hyperactivity disorder). The qualities that allow me to be creative, wild, spontaneous, and playful also make it hard for me to sit still for long periods of time, keep my mouth shut when I am supposed to be "paying attention," and follow through on boring details. At forty-plus years of age, I sometimes still get so excited and exuberant that I cannot contain it. Some people call this a problem of self-regulation. I call it fun.

I make my living by helping ADHD teens succeed in school and by empowering ADHD adults to succeed in their careers and relationships. My ability to infect others with my exuberance is probably my greatest asset in these endeavors, and I owe this to ADHD as well. I have come to see ADHD as a set of traits, a predisposition to confronting life's challenges, and a preference for perceiving the world. I do struggle with many aspects of life because of ADHD, but the older I get, the more I focus on the strengths. My professional training—I am a teacher and ADHD coach with a master's degree in ADHD studies—should have taught me to concentrate on the disorder and pathology of ADHD. Instead, I have become a relentless optimist.

My students and clients have gone to law school and medical school and have started numerous businesses. Many of my clients have proven themselves gifted at sales and marketing. I have witnessed particularly brave ADHDers (people with ADHD) doing some of the world's most dangerous jobs—jobs from which we all benefit but don't have the courage to do ourselves. I have seen teens go from failing grades to the honor roll, because they stopped trying to do school the "right" way and instead found the ADHD way. The ordinary grind of life is particularly hard for ADHDers. Out of necessity, some of us find innovative and creative ways to make life more interesting for ourselves, but we also wind up helping out the whole of humanity in the process.

People with ADHD are often action oriented—which can border on impulsivity—and frequently have a need to take risks. This need, driven by the way the ADHD brain is designed, can cause serious troubles in life. But if we recognize this inclination early in our ADHD young people, we have the chance to harness and develop this precious quality. Risk-takers find shortcuts and more efficient—and fun—ways of carrying out life's tasks. Other ADHDers are more inward focused and possess powers of imagination. Naturally thinking "out of the box," ADHDers possess great potential to find cutting-edge solutions to many of the world's problems.

The trouble is that we have to deal with people and institutions not attuned to the ADHD way. Although the condition has drawbacks and can create setbacks, the greatest handicap is the damage to the belief in ourselves. My professional work has centered on changing this situation. If the families and professionals who come into contact with ADHDers change their mindsets, great things become possible. Drawing from my life experiences and my professional work with ADHDers, this book offers a message of hope. I show you how to appreciate the perceptual, interpersonal, and cerebral preferences of ADHDers. You will see that ADHD imparts many unique strengths and talents and will learn how to work with and develop them. Although offering numerous tools and strategies, this book is a journey into a new way of thinking about yourself and ADHD.

I am a comedian, and humor is found throughout the book. I cannot help it. In lightening up on ADHD, we start to let go of the negative mindset and let in new and energizing ideas that carry transformative power. I want you to have fun as you read this book. Let me be clear: the first priority for you, the reader, is to enjoy yourself.

For those of you who might be a bit more data-oriented, I back up my anecdotes and recommendations with references to contemporary research and scientific understandings of ADHD. I begin the book by discussing my family life and school years, highlighting my struggles and strategies to overcome them. I intersperse my own story with lessons I have learned while working professionally with ADHD people and their families. I particularly focus on mindsets and attitudes. Throughout the book, I provide concrete skills and strategies that ADHDers and their loved ones can use to succeed.

The ultimate goal is to leave you armed with tools and hope for a brighter future. As Russell Barkley, eminent ADHD researcher, has said, the problem with ADHD is that we know what to do, but we do not do what we know. With that wisdom in mind, this book is much less about transmitting information and much more about how to cultivate a hopeful and humor-filled mindset regarding ADHD. What you learn in these pages will challenge you to laugh, think creatively, and follow wisdom that may seem opposite to your instincts. Prepare to hope.

CHAPTER 1

PORTRAIT OF A NORMAL ADHD FAMILY

*"The only problem with the world is
a lot of people don't have ADD."*
Andy Pakula, CEO, Think! Interactive Marketing

FRACTURED FAMILY

My upbringing teemed with intensity. My mother and stepfather had a troubled marriage. There's a shock: a troubled marriage in the 1970s and 1980s in America. Most of their frequent arguments stemmed from my stepfather's absentee and self-centered behavior. He came home from work every night and went straight to his bedroom, where he had a locked army footlocker full of candy, grape soda, and baked goods. He indulged these vices in solitude as he lay in bed watching TV, doing the daily crossword puzzle, and smoking one filterless Chesterfield King cigarette after another. This evening ritual was augmented three to four days a week with a six-pack of beer and a Jack Daniels chaser. Despite having an adult male in the house, my four siblings and I essentially grew up without a father.

My mother's first husband was an Air Force pilot who died when his B-47 bomber crashed. That was in 1964, five years

5

before I was born. She married my father in 1967 and initiated a separation shortly before my birth. Their attempts at reconciliation a year later resulted in the conception and birth of my brother David, who was given up for adoption because my mother wanted nothing to do with my father—he had been physically abusive toward her and my older siblings—and she already had her hands totally full with five children. The prospect of another child was unthinkable. In my mid-twenties, I spent a few years searching for David, and I found him in 1998. Of course, we hadn't grown up together, and I didn't even know about him until I was fifteen. Technically, he is my only full-blooded sibling. Family friends continually remark about the many physical and personality traits he shares with the rest of our family. Just like me, he loves playing practical jokes, has a facility with language, has an incredibly high energy level, and eats with world-record speed. He has been a great gift to everyone in our family.

> *Numerous studies show a strong familial link between ADHD and genetic inheritance. Adoption studies show, for example, higher rates of hyperactivity in the biological parents of hyperactive children than in their adoptive parents.[1] Approximately 15 percent of the ADHD people I see professionally are adopted.*

David laments sometimes about having missed out on growing up with the rest of us. I try to get him to look on the bright side—he never had to meet Tom Kincannon. I was four when my mother married Tom. He was thirty-eight and had never had any children. His parenting style can best be described as the rage-and-withdraw method. We lived in constant chaos. Seven humans, one sheepdog, and a minimum of three cats at any one time were all crammed into a one-thousand-square-foot house, and we frequently took in stray people and pets. Needless to say, peace and quiet were rare commodities.

POOR ME

In my early adult years, I felt I had been deprived. My favorite song was Warren Zevon's "Poor, Poor Pitiful Me." I focused on the negatives and drawbacks of the way I had been raised and saw myself as a victim. "I didn't get enough attention," I would righteously tell myself, or anybody else who would listen. "They didn't love me for who I was." This pity party lasted for several years. I spent thousands of dollars on therapy, workshops, and controlled substances to try to "heal" myself. I practiced yoga, meditation, and kung fu. I joined an evangelical Christian church and travelled as far as the Andes mountains of Peru to work with indigenous shamans. For a time, I shunned most members of my family and blamed them for my unhappiness. I thought that we occupied a special place in the hall of fame of family dysfunction. I thought we had our own wing.

In my mid-twenties, I stopped teaching school—I taught Spanish, French, and Social Studies—and turned my attention to ADHD, a career move that altered the way I thought about my family. In my coaching and counseling work with ADHD young people and adults, I began to get glimpses into the inner workings of other families. Guess what? I realized I was not alone. As I helped my clients wade through family problems, the facades of normalcy that I once envied began to melt away. I peered into the battles that raged in my clients' lives and soon realized that my childhood hadn't actually been that bad. It was bad, just not *that* bad. My siblings all supported me. My mother, unlike the parents of many of the kids that I coach, never tried to control me or get me to conform. This may have been because she loved me or because, with so many kids, she didn't know I existed. I remember asking, "Mom, can I have five dollars to go to the movies?" She said, "Sure, but which one are you?"

Seriously, though, Mom encouraged us to honor our uniqueness. She taught us to believe in ourselves. She modeled creative problem solving and infused us all with a deep sense of tolerance. Mom identified with the underdog. When our financial resources were scarce (and they usually were), she would somehow find money to help other people who were more in need than we were. She taught us to value helping other people more than enriching ourselves. Where I used to see only inadequacy, I began to see a vast reservoir of gifts. Maybe this was just a part of finally growing up.

ADHD: A FAMILY AFFAIR

Everyone in my family—except my oldest sister, Karen—meets at least seven of the ADHD diagnostic criteria. I was pretty sure if you looked for a definition of ADHD in the dictionary, you'd find a picture of my family—a crumpled-up picture, out of focus and with mustard stains, but a picture nonetheless. The many diverse faces of ADHD are well represented. We have our extreme risk-takers, our daydreamers, and our obsessive-compulsive ADHDers. Myself, I am all three at once. I often jump off cliffs while dreaming about moving to California, and I do it over and over and over again.

When I first read a psychiatric description of the condition, I suddenly realized that the way I had grown up was not considered normal. My oldest sister, fourteen years older than I, had figured this out years before. Although prone to many of the same chaotic tendencies as the rest of us, my sister Karen successfully compensated. She put every ounce of her being into managing, controlling, and nurturing her four younger siblings. She was more demanding and had higher expectations of us in many respects than our mother did. She left home at age eighteen but continued to look after us. Karen used to have me over on weekends until I graduated from high school, giving me a much-welcomed and much-needed respite from the dramas of home. I shudder to think where I would be without her constancy in my life.

As much as I see Karen's benevolent impact, I also must admit that I have many times—behind her back—called her a control freak. I think corralling and controlling her siblings is a function etched deep in her brain. The whole family got together for lunch at a restaurant recently, and she tried to supervise where each of us sat. "Kevin," my sister beckoned me in a motherly tone, even though I was forty-one. I still responded like a kid who had just broken an expensive vase in the living room: "What did I do?" My sister continued, "I thought it would be better for you to sit next to the grandchildren, since you're so good at keeping them occupied," which is code for, "You still act like a ten-year-old." Karen has always used compliments to cajole us into submission. She is quite masterful. I stayed right where I was. So did my other siblings when she made similar seating suggestions to them. This push-pull dynamic has always been a source of tension and has frequently erupted into shouting matches, fights, and people stomping their feet and holding their breath until they turned blue.

In case you haven't figured it out already, we are all essentially oppositional-defiant in our family. On some level, we love to bicker and derive pleasure from contradiction. My sister, always the voice of reason and calm, still battles with us for control, but we are an indomitably rebellious lot.

Karen tried to combat many familial traits that she found objectionable. Our loudness was chief among her complaints. IF YOU DIDN'T HEAR ME, OUR LOUDNESS WAS CHIEF AMONG HER COMPLAINTS! She used to talk in hushed and measured tones in an effort to counteract our out-of-control volume. "Maintain low tones," she would whisper to me in a gentle breath. To this day, being around my sister makes me feel like I am back in first grade. In all fairness to Karen, though, every individual in my family thinks that he or she is the only quiet one. We all righteously go around shushing each other, which usually only increases the decibel level. "Don't shush me," I told my sister Wendy at our family Christmas gathering last year. "You're not exactly a church mouse yourself." She shot back, "You just never stop running your mouth, do you?" Can you feel the love?

Each of us also has an insatiable desire to be right. Oddly enough, I'm the only one who always *is* right. Just ask me. The goal is to end an argument on the moral high ground. We are incurable last-word-aholics. Mark my words, as soon as this book is published, one of my siblings will write one. We excel in sarcasm, mockery, and dramatic disdain. These attributes make family gatherings engaging and spirited, if not a bit chaotic.

FAMILY CHAOS

"Go ahead and break it," my mother snarled when my brother Mark threatened to thrust his hand through our family-room window. "You're just hurting yourself." She hoped that reverse psychology would prevent my sixteen-year-old brother from destroying yet another piece of our home. Crash! The glass broke, and blood spurted all over the room. Silence overtook the chaos for a few seconds until I muttered under my breath, "Cool." As the shock abated, my two sisters and mother began to roar in unison, becoming one seamless, outrage-spewing entity. "You've done it again!" my mother screamed. "What did I ever do to deserve this?" Mark was strangely tranquil as he faced this barrage of criticism, as if breaking the glass was a catharsis that allowed him to return to emotional equilibrium. He sat in a chair and said nothing, a look of emptiness on his face. He suffered the verbal beating of the three women without complaint.

> *Although more research is needed, evidence continues to build that ADHD correlates with novelty-seeking genes.[2] Some individuals, like my brother Mark, seem wired to seek out new, perhaps even thrilling, behaviors. If they cannot get this "need" met positively, they will find a way to negatively create the intensity they crave. This tendency can easily be viewed as a character flaw, but harnessed in a positive way, it could well be an evolutionary advantage.*

Mark was the first member of our family to be formally diagnosed with ADHD. My mother took him to clinics across the nation in the late 1960s and early 1970s because local doctors had not helped her get to the bottom of my brother's difficulties, and because it allowed her to get away from the rest of us for a few days at a time. Mark's explosive temper and willingness to focus it on people and objects in our house, as well as at school, made it necessary for him to be sent to a state-run, therapeutic boarding school. Compared with Mark, we all looked pretty normal. He still remains the family scapegoat, and much family drama and discussion center on his misdeeds. If this book doesn't sell well, I'm going to blame it on him.

Mark is a good-hearted person who goes out of his way to help others. He has not done very well, however, at helping himself. He has reading difficulties, which made school unbearably hard. He is a hands-on guy who has trouble sitting still (I am not so different in this regard). He has had one job after another; something always seems to go wrong, usually related to Mark losing his temper. He has not been able to move past the stinging persistence of those early negative messages from school. "I always felt like no matter what I did in school, the teachers would always find something wrong," Mark told me. "I am not sure exactly where it came from, but there was always this reservoir of anger in me. As I've gotten older, I realize that this anger probably came from those early years of school. I just never was able to measure up." Mark failed to perform up to his potential in school and has consistently experienced this as an adult.

Despite his lifelong struggles, he has never wavered in his support and encouragement of me. He bought me clothes and supplied me with lunch money through most of high school. If I have a leak in my roof, Mark comes right over and fixes it. If a motorist is stranded on the side of the road, Mark is the one who will pull over and help. Like many ADHDers, Mark's suffering has paved the way for an uncommonly high level of compassion. I still hope that someday he will take as much care of himself as he does of others. My other siblings and I have done a far better job of keeping our lives together, but we have all struggled, directly or indirectly, because of ADHD.

ON THE WARPATH

I hailed from a household that was bursting with clutter. Making my bed in the morning was a foreign custom to me until I attended summer camp. I still consider making the bed to be a fruitless activity! And what is it with throw pillows on the bed? You buy fancy pillows, put them on your bed in an overlapping and attractive arrangement, and then never use them, not to mention the burden of moving them off the bed every night before going to sleep. Do people say to themselves, "Gee, no one else ever sees these, but when I come into my bedroom and see those beautifully tasseled pillows, it just lifts me up out of my horrible mood"? Anyway, my mother was savvy enough never to try to introduce this concept at our house. We were lucky if we had a clean towel.

Cleaning the house occurred at irregular intervals whenever my sister Wendy went on the "warpath." Wendy sometimes became disgusted at what a "pigsty" the house had become. Her irritation would build until finally she would punish all of us by cleaning the house. Gritting her teeth and snarling, she would bombard us with warnings like "I'm on the warpath; you better all leave now. There's no telling what I'm capable of." We would gladly leave; she would concentrate her massive amount of ADHD energy, and we would return to a sparklingly clean house, which would stay that way for about two hours. Luckily, she had few emotional reserves left to resist us after her incredible domestic undertaking. We were grateful that she cleaned the house, because it gave us something to do, something we were good at: messing it up again.

Like Wendy, my brother Gerard also became disgusted with—and embarrassed by—our house. One summer when he was fifteen, he decided to work on our landscaping. As he tells the story, "My friend Johnny and I hooked up chains to Mom's Camaro and pulled out all of the bushes one night." To find replacements, Gerard and Johnny went out late at night and dug up bushes from various houses in the area, replanting them in front of our house before sunrise. One shrub came from Mr. MacArdle's house, which was on the corner of our street. This man was chief among our neighborhood's numerous lawn Nazis. Gerard decided to dig up Mr. MacArdle's rare, three-branched bush that looked like a topiary from the Palace of Versailles. At least my brother had good taste. Of course, Mr. MacArdle discovered the shrubbery caper the next day as he drove down the street after work. Luckily, he simply demanded that my brother transplant the bush back in his yard, and if it lived, pledged no further action. It lives still!

I, however, accepted the fact that tidiness and organization were not valued in our household and, until I went to high school, had no shame about the state of our messy abode. My room was so messy that you could walk across the floor and never have your feet touch the carpet. When Wendy went on the "warpath," I would come home to find on my bed everything that had been on the floor. It was actually a simple, sixty-second task to return the room to its former state. Ninth grade marked a turning point, as friends of mine who visited the house began to remark to me and then to others how unbelievably cluttered and unkempt our household was. As adolescence moved forward, I became self-conscious about other aspects of my family as well.

BETTER LATE THAN NEVER

My family's lack of promptness made us fodder for gossip. Because Mom exhibited many ADHD traits, all of us kids resigned ourselves to the necessity of lying to her about pickup times for sports, school, and other activities. A 5:30 end time for baseball practice, for example, meant having to tell my mother 4:15 if we wanted a sporting chance of getting picked up on time. During particularly stressful times for my mother, if we wanted to be picked up by 6:00 on Friday, we had to tell her 3:30 the prior Wednesday. She'd still be late, but at least we'd make it home in time for Saturday morning cartoons. Mrs. Lahaut, my tee-ball coach, was generous enough to drop me off on her way home. I am sure she was doing this mostly for her own benefit, so she did not have to wait for my mother. Parties and gatherings always saw our family arrive last. Some people didn't mind, because at least we were there to help clean up.

Mom frequently panicked right before it was time to leave the house. "Oh, we can't leave yet, kids," she would say with alarm. "The kitty litter needs to be changed and the dishes are piling up." Never mind that she had spent the whole day talking on the phone and the kitty litter had needed attention for well over a week. She created a crisis in her mind in those moments, which made us late so consistently that no one ever expected us on time.

> *Procrastination, although often an annoying and self-sabotaging behavior, can serve to increase cerebral arousal.[3] ADHDers often talk about needing intensity to get motivated to work. Although it may always seem like an unproductive behavior, leaving things until the last minute creates a crisis, which then creates the levels of neurotransmitters and cerebral arousal needed to stimulate the brain enough to focus on the task. This is why many ADHDers function well in jobs that require crisis and intensity.*

Our family had its own timetable for transitioning from one activity to another. In addition to arriving late and leaving early, we all took showers that often completely drained the hot water heater. My sister Wendy had the nasty habit of picking the bathroom lock and pouring a pan of cold water on whoever was in the shower when she was ready to bathe. The one bathroom in our house was a constant combat zone. My mother fought with us every morning to wake up and every evening to go to bed. We were all night owls by nature, and most of us still are. We have very different rhythms than most other people in the world.

ADDICTS AND ENABLERS

Even more serious than our struggles with daily routines, substance abuse runs rampant in our family. I mean every substance: drugs, alcohol, sugar, salt, and junk food. ADHD individuals are at an increased risk of becoming addicts.[4] My family has equal complements of addicts and the "helpers" who unconsciously allow addicts to continue their destructive ways. My mother and her only sister married men who were alcoholics. Both these women were more or less teetotalers who preached the evils of alcohol. My mother dealt with my stepfather's addiction as an enabler and a fixer. She married him knowing that he had a drinking problem, and she honestly believed that she could cure him. He had convinced her that a wife and kids were just what he needed to motivate him to stop drinking. He was also in debt, and it didn't hurt that she owned a house.

My mother told me recently that she really thought she was doing the right thing by marrying him. She not only got a husband out of the deal, as she recalls, but she was doing a Christian deed. "I thought he was a great guy," she admitted with a tinge of embarrassment. "I thought God had brought him to me so that I could help him and so that he could help us all [the family]." She almost broke down in tears at that point, and I felt bad for even bringing the issue up. "I was a fool," she said.

My mother bailed him out of jail. She made excuses to his friends, coworkers, and family when alcohol impaired his ability to live up to his responsibilities. After they married, she paid off some of his bills and put his name on her house. She tolerated physical violence on many occasions when he would beat one of my siblings—occasions that are horrifically etched in my mind. I thank God that I was spared my stepfather's wrath. I became a people-pleasing "good boy" so that his rage was never focused on me. I started making him breakfast in bed when I was nine years old. He scared me to my core.

Mom took great pains to make it look as though everything was all right in our house. But she could only hide so much.

Luckily, in our neighborhood, we were not that unusual. One neighbor, Dorothy Brady, divorced her alcoholic husband, giving my mother the idea to do the same. She threatened but never followed through.

My mother's only sister married a successful businessman. Uncle Ralph was an alcoholic and a gambler. My cousin Robert tells of his mother putting him and his siblings to bed early on nights when she knew their father would be coming home drunk. She stayed with Ralph until his untimely death, but she busied herself maintaining an air of normalcy in their upper-middle-class, suburban life. Let's be honest. As I discovered later on, this *was* a normal upper-middle-class suburban life.

Before my uncle died, he and my aunt migrated to Las Vegas, a move most people chalked up to Uncle Ralph's desire to be close to the center of the gambling universe. When he died prematurely of a heart attack, he left my aunt a sizable gambling debt.

My father's brother, also a gambler, was an itinerant alcoholic who roamed the country and left a few fatherless children along the way. My father weighed more than 400 pounds but was reluctant to admit he had a problem, claiming, "I just do not get my proper exercise." Yeah, for like the previous forty-three years. He died in 2008 of a massive heart attack at age sixty-six. Both sides of my family are replete with addicts.

Among my siblings and cousins, alcohol addiction and marijuana use have been a problem. My cousin John is a crack addict who has put our whole family through years of tragedy. Last year, his mother told me that he had found the PIN for her ATM card and stole more than eight thousand dollars to feed his habit. If you know anything about crack addicts, that's a pretty small amount. Neither his siblings nor his cousins allow him at family gatherings. Although John's mother has attended Al-Anon to work on her enabling issues, she did not report this incident to the police and continues to let him into her house. On the other hand, there's nothing left because he stole it all, so why not let him in?

Owing to a streak of good fortune and powerful mentors, I

never became a substance addict. I credit the constant reminders from my mother, the powerful support from my sisters, and extraordinary mentoring from a long line of influential role models.

CYBER JUNKIE

Although I did dodge the bullet of substance abuse, I succumbed to another addiction that ADHDers are increasingly struggling with: I am a recovering cyber addict. I wasted years of my life staring at a computer screen and as a result achieved none of my goals, except for the international high score on *Ms. Pac Man*, and I'm proud of that. I felt pangs of guilt and sadness after video gaming binges that lasted for weeks, but not enough guilt to get me to stop. After ten hours playing or chatting online, I would rationalize, "Hey, at least I'm not doing crack!" I hid my behavior from everyone for almost ten years and refused to admit the problem to myself. In 2003, I hit bottom. I realized my life was out of control. When I finally admitted I had a problem, I was overcome with disgust at myself. After longing for many years to be a writer, perform stand-up comedy, and have a band, I realized I had done absolutely nothing with my talents.

I obsessively used the computer because, like most ADHDers, the ordinary routines of life wear me down. I used the computer and the Internet to avoid facing my problems and to escape reality. I lacked direction in my life, and instead of trying to find my path, I pursued adventure and fulfillment in the cyber world. It seemed to work out fine for Bill Gates, but not for me. The only reason my first book, *Cyber Junkie: Escape the Gaming and Internet Trap*, got written was that I came out of denial and found support to finally deal with my problem.

WE NEED NEW IDEAS

The cyber world gives me a constant stream of new stimulation, offering me something that most ADHDers crave: novelty.

Neurotransmitter and activation levels in the ADHD brain are lower than in the non-ADHD brain, so we need new stimuli and excitement to turn on our brains.[5] ADHDers have trouble sustaining alertness, and activities that are highly stimulating make it easier to stay alert.[6] As familiarity with a setting or task increases, the ability to stay alert decreases.[7]

In my family, we all tend toward exuberance and excitement at the inception of an idea, but quickly lose steam, and therefore do not usually possess the wherewithal to bring that idea to fruition once the luster of novelty wears off. We exhibit such passion and brilliance at the start of an endeavor; one would never dream that a few days later all would be lost and no further energy would be expended in pursuit of the goal. I remember watching an episode of *The Brady Bunch* in which Peter Brady builds a volcano for a school science project. It just so happened that I was in need of an idea at that time for my own seventh-grade science project. I saw it clearly in my mind's eye from the moment that Peter made the volcano erupt all over his sister Marcia and her friends. I saw the glory that would be mine when I revealed my own volcano to the class, how the teacher and the other kids would marvel at my genius. I could see that eruption as clearly as if I were on top of Mount Pinatubo, but I had no idea what steps were necessary to complete such a complex feat. More importantly, *I had no clue* that I had no idea about the steps to follow, so I couldn't even ask for help. Clinicians would highlight my problems in "executive functioning," and "working memory."[8] My many experiences up to that point should have shown me that I needed to plan in order to complete the project, but I had not integrated past experience enough to alter my choices. I let my volcanic euphoria carry me along and never did manage to arrive at a finished project. For me, the juice was at the inception of an idea, not at its completion.

My mother modeled a lack of perseverance, setting an example that my siblings and I were to follow. Many a charlatan made his or her way into Mom's life, often ensnaring her by extolling her abilities as a consummate people person. Mom has managed to involve herself in many a get-rich-quick scheme as well as several "promising" independent business ventures. Into this latter category we must put Mom's more than thirty-year involvement with Mary Kay cosmetics. This corporation boasted that it, in my mother's words, "helped women take charge of their lives." From our family's perspective, the company's promises were wholly unrealized, and Mom's futile forays into the cutthroat world of retail cosmetics left her with less energy and fewer resources to spend on us. Mom used to go to the yearly "Jamborees" for the company in Dallas and was treated to pep talks from the likes of sales icon Zig Ziglar; she even got to spend some personal time with Mary Kay Ash herself. The weeks after those events would witness Mom spending furious hours on the phone setting up facials and home parties and exhibiting the kind of determination that might have made her a success. Those rare bursts of intense focus typically petered out in less than a month. The last venture Mom engaged in revolved around a "laundry ball," some "magical" laundry cleaning device that worked through electrostatic attraction. When we asked her specific questions about science when we were kids, she would often reply, "Mama's not good at science, dear." With the laundry ball, however, she had suddenly become an enthusiastic expert in electromagnetism. This went on for about two months, until she figured out that the laundry wasn't getting clean and her customers started to complain.

LIKE MOTHER, LIKE SON

The apple doesn't fall far from the tree; I, too, have allowed myself to be taken in by many network marketing schemes, in which a few reap enormous rewards and many (let's be honest, most) end up losing money. I set out to make my fortune with programs designed by companies like Amway, Primerica, and Arbonne, and lost time and money with each one. (By the way, if you ever want to buy any soap or cosmetics, I still have a garage full of the stuff.) I accept full responsibility and do not blame these companies. I do believe, however, that most network marketing companies thrive on people like us. We ADHDers are prone to be taken in by the initial whirlwind of possibilities for financial independence, personal freedom, and an easy buck. But most of us lack follow-through and have trouble sustaining our motivation.

I was certainly not showing the ability to learn from past failure when I spent two weeks trying to sell the "amazing" Rainbow vacuum. (It really is a great machine, just insanely expensive.) I will never forget how excited I was that first week, pumped up with the prospect of helping America rid itself of dust and allergens and revolutionizing the way people cleaned their homes. Forget about the fact that my family rarely cleaned house and that I had never used a vacuum before. I vigorously made appointments with members of my extended family and several family friends to demonstrate this remarkable "home cleaning system." I figured I had sat through hundreds of their sales pitches for "technologically advanced" knife sets, handy-dandy vegetable slicers, and food dehydrators that were supposed to transform America's kitchens. I made no sales. I had no chance with the people in my family. They were either apathetic about cleaning or suffered sales exhaustion from long-term exposure to other gimmicks and schemes proffered by other members of my family over many decades. They had all been subjected to numerous clever sales pitches. These people wouldn't even buy raffle tickets for school. What chance did I have with a thousand-dollar vacuum? That was a lot of money in 1988.

Another side to the story is that people in my family, like many ADHDers, are drawn to schemes like this because we value our independence and bristle at authority. If some of this tendency is hardwired into us, our experiences in school certainly help bring it out. We tend not to fit in well with systems that other people have created, such as school, jobs, laws, governments, and the planet Earth. We prefer to be on our own, but often lack the skills that we need to be independently successful. I have managed to be a successfully self-employed person, but only after learning lessons from several failures and hiring a coach to help me apply those lessons in my daily life. It also doesn't hurt that I work with ADHD folks. They are much more forgiving of my flaws than the general population. Even when they are not forgiving, they quickly forget!

THE OTHER SIDE OF THE COIN

I think the most important reason for my success in helping ADHDers succeed is my family. I may not have learned to color-coordinate my clothes, organize my room, or brush my teeth regularly, but my house was the perfect laboratory environment to train me for my future career. I dealt with almost every conceivable type of ADHD right in my own home. I have an effortless appreciation for the subtleties and nuances of the condition. As I sit with new clients, I am always amazed at how their stories feel so close to my own. For me, ADHD is a normal way of being in the world that offers many, often untapped, gifts. I thank my family and upbringing for this awareness.

In spite of what might be considered liabilities, our house stood as a hub of neighborhood activity. Everyone wanted to be part of our orbit because we always had a good time. Exciting possibilities brewed at our house. Some of these possibilities involved broken bones and trips to emergency rooms, but man, were they fun. We organized massive water-balloon fights throughout the neighborhood. Many of these became, quite literally, mud-slinging matches. When my parents were away, we had wild and memorable parties. In preparation for those parties, we buried our differences by uncharacteristically teaming up to thoroughly clean the house.

My mother was always willing to include as many kids as possible whenever we went somewhere. We would regularly have a carload of neighborhood children as we drove to parades, sporting events, and amusement parks. On one occasion, she took a group of my friends and me to a speech by Jimmy Carter, who was president at the time. OK, they weren't all fun, but you have to sleep sometime. You never knew what was going to happen with our family.

Our spontaneity made us popular. My mother's often unorthodox views and her nonjudgmental nature also endeared her to neighborhood youngsters. She welcomed stray animals and stray teenagers alike. Many young people spent time at our house because they could not talk to their own parents. My mother offered a friendly ear and dispensed sympathetic advice. (My older brother dispensed loose joints behind the garage, but that's another matter.) I regularly run into people I grew up with who recount the important role my mother played in their lives. Last week at a speech I gave on cyber addictions, I ran into John Frank, a neighbor of ours, who remembered myriad ways my mother had influenced his life. "She always said, 'Be more Christian,'" John told me. "That always stuck with me, and I have used it with my own kids. Your mother always taught kindness and acceptance toward others."

She also helped a long line of down-on-their-luck adults, often by marrying them. We had Chuck Tank living with us for two years. He was a career alcoholic with throat cancer whom my mother and sister nursed and nurtured until he died. We had Dickie Brown living in our basement for six months. He was a hard-drinking and pugnacious neighborhood ruffian who had lost his house. My mother's friends were aghast that she allowed such a "beast" to move in. Mom knew how to tame him, though, and for years afterward Dickie would stop by to see if there were any odd jobs around the house he could do for her, and to look behind the garage to see if my brother had missed any "roaches." My mother taught me that no one was beyond help and that it was our duty to take care of the less fortunate, which also kept us from focusing excessively on our own problems. My mother's resilience allowed her to keep a positive attitude through many challenges: the death of the love of her life (her first husband), an abusive husband, an alcoholic husband, giving up a child for adoption, and raising five children on her own. Outside observers could have easily identified shortcomings in my mother, but the older I get, the more I see strength.

I was raised thinking that I was normal and that I had something powerful to give to others. We certainly were a picture-perfect dysfunctional family, but my mother honored our differences, and, quite understandably I think, my siblings and I thought most other families we encountered were just plain dull. I may have received shaming and belittling messages from the world at large, but in my home I was surrounded by individuals who found absolute joy in idiosyncrasies and delighted in characteristics that others labeled weird, inappropriate, and perhaps even unacceptable.

ADHD definitely has a strong genetic component, but this does not detract from the incredible role that environment and upbringing play. I am thoroughly convinced that my family made me feel normal, in spite of a constant stream of negative messages from the outside world. Research is now showing that the responses of parents, peers, and teachers to an ADHDer play a powerful role in how the individual develops.[9] While more than 50 percent of ADHD individuals struggle with addictions, roughly 50 percent do not. It is important to look into why almost half of us do not.[10] I suspect positive family support plays a key role. In spite of school experiences that had me feeling inadequate and flawed, my family gave me a core belief that my way of being in the world was totally OK. In the last thirteen years, my mission has been to take this message to the rest of the world.

CHAPTER 2

THE WORLD IS
FALLING APART

"Pessimism never won any battle."
President Dwight D. Eisenhower

PROFILES IN FRUSTRATION

People who spend a lot of time with ADHDers often develop an attitude that I call "The World Is Falling Apart." They are sure that a horrible future awaits the ADHDer in his or her life. They focus on the negative eventualities they think are certain to occur. They settle into a routine of expressing their well-founded concerns about our slim prospects for a happy future.

As an unforeseen consequence, the relationship with the ADHDer in their lives tends to have a palpable negative twinge. Although the worrying and perseverating derives from genuine care for their ADHD loved one, this mindset does not help us ADHDers all that much, and it certainly does not help the person who lives his or her life in inner turmoil, constantly focusing on the darker sides of ADHD. The capacity for parents and loved ones of ADHDers to creatively prognosticate doom and gloom never ceases to surprise me, and it is even a bit entertaining. A few years ago I began taking notes on this tendency and have amassed volumes of anecdotes.

Mothers often reflect on the contentious relationship they have with their ADHD children. They naturally wonder, given the incessant arguments they put up with, how on earth he or she could possibly have a positive relationship as an adult. At one of my workshops entitled "Lightening Up on ADHD," one mother voiced concerns that were shared by many in attendance: "What is he going to do when he gets married? Is his wife going to get him up every morning, find his keys and wallet, and then call his boss to make up a creative excuse as to why he's late yet again?" Several mothers nodded in agreement and felt a much-needed sense of support that they were not alone.

Many parents worry about prospects for marriage, but almost all parents with an ADHD child express fear that he or she will grow up to be serially unemployed. They assume, perhaps not incorrectly, that constant struggles with homework will assuredly translate into troubles in the office down the road. Jim, the father of an eleven-year-old girl whom I was trying to help succeed in school, was clearly at his wits' end when we met for the first time. "I lose sleep every single night thinking about her future," he told me. "The only job I can think of for my daughter when she gets older is a magician who specializes in disappearing acts . . . because once homework begins, the pencils, pens, clipboard, and anything else that's needed seem to vanish into thin air." The massive amount of energy his daughter put into *not* doing the homework drove Jim crazy. To make matters worse, Jim's wife also has ADHD, which is not surprising since ADHD tends to run in families. She, too, has lost many things, including her diamond engagement ring!

Forgotten tasks and lost articles cause a great deal of stress in every household that has an ADHDer. While Jim's daughter hides the backpack and school supplies, Kathy's nine-year-old son hides himself. "He hides in the closet to avoid doing homework," she said. "This kid actually enjoys the closet. He has snacks in there and even has his Game Boy to keep him company, when he manages to steal it back from me." I, like many ADHD adults, used to hide in front of my computer screen, playing games, not answering my phone for hours on end, and disengaging from the world.

Some ADHDers string their parents, or spouses, along by promising that after one more game, or one more TV show, they will gladly begin their work. Sue, who attended one of my "lightening up" workshops, described her son as "The Minute Man." She told us, "Everything is 'in a minute,' but the minute never comes. Are there jobs for people like this? Indefinitely delaying work—is this a marketable skill?" I informed her that union organizers did employ this tactic from time to time. It's called "The Slow Down."

Ron, a thirty-seven-year-old ADHDer who participates in one of my cyber addiction recovery groups, put up with incessant nagging growing up and married a woman to whom his mother passed that torch. He first came to the group because his wife threatened to divorce him if he didn't get his *World of Warcraft* playing under control. Our minds crave the shifting stimulation of video games and TV. After spending all day working to stay focused in a world that seems ill-suited to us, it's often too tempting to plug in to an electronic world that seems to vibrate on our same frequency. A large percentage of the people who come to me for help with cyber addictions also have ADHD.

Although getting their ADHD loved one to do chores and homework bedevils many families, the penchant for risk-taking that some ADHDers have can lead to truly serious consequences. Marcie and Tom worried that their son would someday blow up their house. Tom mused, "I wish that creativity in working with fire was the start of a solid career path. Last week, I went to the backyard and found my fourteen-year-old son with a can of hair spray in his right hand and a lighter in his left. He was playing a game he calls 'flame thrower.' Luckily, he only singed a few bushes this time."

Fran and Al, another couple with an ADHD risk-taker, seemed proud when they told me, "He's been to the emergency room so many times that he knows the doctors and nurses by name." The couple had actually been encouraging their son to follow what seemed to be a fitting career path. Fran had thought about it extensively. "I now believe," Fran said, "that my son would make a great stuntman. I became convinced of this when he was six and put on a cape to play Superman by repeatedly jumping off the garage. He didn't learn from trial and error, though. I think he thought there was a chance he was actually going to fly if he just kept at it long enough. His sky-high tolerance for pain flabbergasts me!"

Paul, a fifty-year-old doctor with ADHD, has broken eleven bones and been hospitalized four times in the last ten years for injuries sustained while engaging in extreme sports. In spite of his wife's protests, Paul continues his Evel Knievel lifestyle and shows no signs of slowing down. "He seems to have a need to take ridiculous risks," his wife told me. "Is there any way to get him to stop?"

A recent study of children and adolescents with ADHD found a strong tendency for ADHDers to overestimate their physical abilities, intentionally take unnecessary risks, and anticipate positive or no consequences from their behavior.[1] It is well documented that people with ADHD are more likely to be injured in an accident, "with up to 57% being described as accident-prone and 15% having had at least four or more serious accidental injuries, such as broken bones, lacerations, head injuries, severe bruises, lost teeth, or accidental poisonings."[2]

Part of the problem with our risk-taking is that we have trouble seeing the consequences that may result. Research points to this inability as deriving from abnormalities and underactivity in several parts of the brain,[3] while multiple genes seem to predispose certain individuals to novelty-seeking—in other words, risk-taking—behavior.[4] Failure to factor in likely consequences also plays a role in lying, an area in which many ADHDers, like me, excel. "He lies even when he doesn't have to," Linda told me, frustrated. "Why does my son make up such stories?"

Carol has an ADHD son who has the makings of a great writer. He weaves fantastic, but somewhat believable, stories at will. Carol has received calls from other parents congratulating her for winning the lottery, offering condolences for supposedly dead relatives, and wondering if her nephew had recovered from his hiking accident on Mount McKinley. She told a group of parents and me, "My ten-year-old ADHD son does not understand that making up such stories is usually inappropriate. Last week, he told his friend's mother that he had to go to the hospital to visit his cousin who had been bitten by a black widow spider. There was no truth to the story at all. Do ADHD people ever go into politics?"

I used to make up stories too. I was good at it and found that the more outlandish details I included, the more kids were interested in what I had to say. I used lying not only to evade punishment and scorn, but also just to get attention. I felt like a social misfit, almost always out of step with my peers. Lying allowed me to create a phantom life that made me seem, at least in my mind, much more interesting. Of course, the greatest lies I told were to myself.

START A PROJECT THE NIGHT BEFORE

Through most of my school years, I figured out how to copy, cheat, and lie with great success. As I mentioned previously, I had to do a science project in seventh grade that involved constructing a working volcano. I started the night before and realized that there was absolutely no way to complete it. I decided to make up a sob story. This is when I realized just how good I was at acting. The next day, I went to school early to talk to the teacher and recounted a tale of addiction, family violence, and mayhem. I was in tears by the end, and my teacher allowed me to do a makeup project. She even believed me when I told her that I would get into deep trouble if she uttered one word to anyone in my family. I then hugged her and thanked her profusely. She allowed me to stay after school for a few weeks to help her in the science classroom and then didn't count the science project when figuring the final grade. I ended up with a B+, which upset me greatly—with that story, I should have gotten an A! Actually, I was elated, and I never bragged about my achievement. I knew if I bragged, it would get back to the teacher. I had the makings of a successful pathological liar.

I, like many ADHD individuals, had a seemingly innate capacity for lying. My theory is that this capacity develops because we have the experience of teachers, parents, and people in authority yelling at us and criticizing us. Our "shame tanks," our capacity to receive shaming messages, get full and we just can't take any more, so we lie to avoid being told that we're not good enough.[5] We consistently hear the same sorts of things:

- "Can't you just behave?"
- "What were you thinking?"
- "What's the matter with you?"
- "Are you out of your mind?"
- "Are you stupid?"
- "Well, once again you didn't use your brains!"
- "I can't take this anymore."
- "Why are the police at the front door?"
- "Do you realize how long that vase was in our family?"
- "No one else wears their underwear on the outside of their pants."
- "You used my toothbrush for *what*?"

In our hearts, we start to believe that something is seriously wrong with us, and this sense often becomes so overwhelming that we just can't take it any longer. We think we're bad people, and no human being can easily live with that. We lie to protect our fragile psyches.

When parents and loved ones have to constantly deal with their ADHDer's deception, refusals to do homework and chores around the house, and intent to risk life and limb, it is no wonder parents and loved ones can become negative and stay that way. During the last few years, I have tried through a series of workshops to help pull them out of that mindset. One seminar, "Fun with ADHD: A Parent's Guide To Humor," helped inspire this book. Those who try to help us quite understandably get stuck in negativity, and they do not know how to get out. But they really want to.

> *Cognizant of the stress of having an ADHD family member, most researchers and practitioners recommend parent and spousal training to learn effective relational techniques.*[6] *The national ADHD support organization Children and Adults with Attention Deficit/Hyperactivity Disorder (CHADD) offers a "Parent-to-Parent" training that can provide great support and information.*

THE WHOLE TRUTH

I cannot sugarcoat ADHD. It has drawbacks. My innate imagination and spontaneity are counterbalanced by an interminable struggle with boredom and life-altering lapses of follow-through. I still have a low grade on my college transcript because I was late submitting paperwork to prove that I was sick for the final exam (I really was!). In fact, I still have not turned it in. The professor left the country for a five-year stint working in sub-Saharan Africa after that semester, and I still have not managed to track her down. I had an A in the class going into that final. I am still irritated at the "injustice" of it all, even though I accept full responsibility. I have never changed anything in my life without accepting responsibility for the choices I have made. If I forget a commitment or responsibility, I have trained myself to say that I "chose to not remember." When I can see and accept the choice that I made, I come one step closer to being able to make a different decision next time.

For many years, I blamed everybody but myself for my failures and consequently ended up repeating many of the same mistakes. When the mistakes began piling up, I started engaging in failure avoidance, pulling back from life so that I could control the sting of disappointment. The 14,000 hours I racked up on computer games over ten years highlight the fact that I have spent a lot of energy engaging in escapism, eschewing my problems instead of confronting them.

Many of my ADHD clients and students are also escapists. They come to me because they are not living up to their academic or professional potential. In a remarkably high percentage of cases, they are cyber junkies, substance abusers, or both. Some of them use marijuana to reduce their anxiety, constructing elaborate rationalizations on its medicinal value. Others justify their eight-to-ten-hour-a-day video game habit by deluding themselves into thinking they will turn professional, becoming one of the very few people in the world who make money playing video games. ADHDers become adept at deflecting criticism and resist efforts to get them to identify and own up to destructive behaviors, most of which are rooted in growing up in families and societies that do not understand and honor those with this condition. Many if not most of us experience failure so many times that we construct layers of defenses for purposes of self-preservation. It is very difficult to repeatedly get the message that "Something is wrong with you!"

Self-deception and a lack of personal accountability were my two greatest barriers to success. I could not deal with my problems until I admitted they existed. I could not change the circumstances of my life until I accepted responsibility for creating them. For so many years, I denied that anything was wrong. As far as school was concerned, I felt flawed both academically and socially, but for the most part I suffered in silence. Some powerful inner impulse resisted anything that might result in my actually feeling that sense of inadequacy.

I am honestly discussing my struggles in order to highlight the strategies I have used to succeed. I want to demonstrate that it is possible to live with ADHD and still achieve one's dreams. The first step toward success is simply admitting one's part in creating failure.

Once a person can see his or her role in a situation, change becomes possible. For every ADHDer, radical self-honesty is indispensable. I will follow my own advice by disclosing something I have tried most of my adult life to hide: I am a slob.

PILES, PILES EVERYWHERE!

I, like almost all ADHDers, have always had difficulty dealing with large amounts of paper. And by large amounts of paper, I do not mean large amounts of money; I never seem to have enough of that. As I sit here at my computer, I am surrounded by a veritable mountain range of files, documents, bills, and other "interesting" papers I hang on to. I have a shoe box on one corner of the desk that contains nothing but business cards I have collected over the last fifteen years. It is almost full, and once a card goes in there, it never comes out. I have shoe boxes of everything, except shoes. I have an unopened box with a heart rate monitor I bought three years ago, stacks of newspaper articles that I cut out but never read, and four rarely used dictionaries. By the way, if you had read this manuscript before my editor got hold of it, you'd know how rarely I use those dictionaries. Somewhere under this mess lies a Palm Pilot that my brother generously gave me for Christmas several years ago. He really thought, bless his heart, that it "would help organize" my life. He didn't understand that for it to organize my life, I would have to at least open the box!

Many people would feel ashamed of the chaos I regularly live with, and I guess I do, too, but I also revel in the rare skill that it takes to balance my piles without them falling over. Ned Hallowell calls piles the "kudzu of ADD."[7] I get irritated if someone tries to move something or combine my "kudzu" without proper authorization. "Those are my piles," I told the cleaning lady. "Don't mess with them!" She only lasted two weeks, because she organized things so well that I had trouble finding several important items, like my car keys, socks, underwear, pants, bed, and the house where I lived. Filing my papers or sifting through them without being motivated by some crisis never crosses my mind.

As I now survey the jumbled mess on my desk, the scattered and perplexing tangle of papers mirrors the often scattered state of my mind. I have struggled throughout my life with keeping track of what I have considered small details: doctors' appointments, financial documents, bank statements, my passport (which I have lost three times), large amounts of cash—I have even lost a good number of checks paid to me by my clients. (Usually I do not tell them because I am embarrassed, and I silently suffer the loss. Some of them have actually figured this out and say once in a while, "I gave you a check; don't you remember?") Details elude me. I pay little attention to what I instinctually interpret as "inconsequential" minutiae. You know, what other people call the important stuff.

HELP! I'VE FALLEN AND I CAN'T GET UP!

My workshop offerings obviously have their root in my belief that people take ADHD way too seriously. Of course, we have to be serious to a certain extent. But as Czech writer Vaclav Havel noted, "Anyone who takes himself too seriously always runs the risk of looking ridiculous; anyone who can consistently laugh at himself does not." We have to have balance, something hard to attain with an ADHDer around. After years of dealing with concerned and angry parents who bring their kids to see me in my capacity as an ADHD coach, I am convinced that the negativity of loved ones is one of the biggest problems. By and large, before they come to see me, family members try a number of different approaches, none of which seem to offer significant benefit. A severe and persistent hopelessness takes root. One mother of ADHD children put it this way:

> I'm not sure when I began to question my sanity. I had known for some time that my life was unmanageable. It was clear

that my children were the focal point of the chaos that had become my everyday experience. I had explored every avenue, read every book, and talked to every professional available. I had attended doctor's appointments without end, therapy sessions without merit, lectures by nonbelievers, and had been subjected to countless hours of . . . advice. After all that, I still only knew one thing: my children had attention-deficit/ hyperactivity disorder.[8]

This story is quite typical of family members I have encountered in my professional practice. When I meet families the first time, it usually does not take long for the immense frustration to rear its head.

Maggie was a devoted mother who spent every waking hour trying to help Christina, her ADHD daughter. A registered nurse with a master's degree in public policy, Maggie stopped working when Christina started high school. She gave up her career to help her daughter dig her way out of Ds and Fs in school. Her unflagging devotion was largely responsible for Christina going from failing most classes in ninth grade to a 2.9 grade point average by her senior year. Maggie did not, however, know how to let go. She was going to keep hammering away until her daughter was successful in every area. She never let Christina forget the sacrifices she had made, hoping, I am sure, to motivate Christina through guilt.

Maggie seemed oblivious to the destructive impact of her overbearing nature. Although she ostensibly came to me so that I could help Christina, I asked myself at our very first meeting, *I wonder if this woman has ever wondered if* she's *part of the problem?* When I asked Maggie what issues we needed to work on, she steamrolled me with a litany of what seemed to be petty complaints. I was particularly shocked when she immodestly shared her daughter's bathroom behaviors: "She is seventeen and still hasn't learned to flush the toilet every time." When I unwisely suggested that this issue was somewhat unimportant, I received a lesson on the darker side of the female world. Maggie gravely told me, "You don't know what women are like. She will be the butt of every joke in the office. The other women will know it's her, and they'll think she's dirty and nasty and won't talk to her." I quickly drew that sharing episode to a close. Maggie had a hard time shifting gears and repeatedly brought up the toilet issue during that and other meetings.

I do not wish to underplay the importance of bathroom etiquette, but Maggie exemplifies the black hole that loved ones of ADHDers can fall into. Small victories in the past had given them hope, but on many occasions their ADHD loved ones had snatched defeat from the jaws of victory. Hope becomes a luxury that these people do not allow themselves, because hope makes it harder to bear the eventual fall that they are sure will come calling again. The interpersonal dynamic suffers as families become mired in negativity, nastiness, and nay-saying.

KNEE-JERK REACTIONS

When I am asked whether I think I can help a young person, I always begin the process by scheduling a meeting with both the child and the parents. I ask spouses or significant others to attend when dealing with adult clients. I view this as an opportunity for us to interview each other and see whether we think a working relationship is possible. What starts off as a routine discussion of strengths and weaknesses usually devolves into volleys of accusations, hurt feelings, and emotional shutdown. In these initial meetings with families, I have often felt relegated to the role of referee. This is familiar territory for me, given my argument-prone family. In my early years as an ADHD coach dealing with these exchanges, I tended to take the side of the ADHDer. I struggled to maintain balance.

I asked thirteen-year-old Ryan several questions during the initial meeting I had with him and his parents. Each and every time, he got out about three words and then both of his parents would interrupt, almost in unison. I remember thinking, *I wouldn't do my homework either if I had these two breathing down my neck every day.* I had to use one of my favorite tricks to get the parents to lay off a bit. "For the rest of this meeting, I am Ryan's attorney," I told them. "Please do not talk directly to my client." I made a joke out of it, which helped lighten up the mood, and the parents did abide by my wishes.

I was not so lucky with Hank, a police detective whose rage at his son was obvious from the moment the two of them entered my office. Every time I suggested Hank needed to back off, he would share another of his son's transgressions, seemingly to justify his own rage. I took the side of the son, and I remember actually being afraid of Hank and thinking, *I had better not sit too close, because this man might hit me.* I foolishly suggested that Hank might have some ADHD issues himself. The rage then came out full force as he told me, "You're just like the teachers, psychologists, and everybody else. Blame the parents! Blame the parents! Blame the parents!"

I, in my ignorance and well-scrubbed self-righteousness, started off my career by unabashedly blaming. This allowed me to be the savior, the rescuer. Twelve years of Catholic school had taught me to relish that role. I was the one who would swoop down and save the day. At that point, November 1998, I did not have enough professional exposure to understand the complex family dynamics that ADHD creates. I had little appreciation for the predicament of the parents and spouses. Hank was right. I definitely blamed them.

LIVING IN THE LAND OF THE "JUST"

Blaming the parents is a fairly common incorrect assumption and accusation. People who have never spent long periods of time with an ADHDer have no idea what it's like. Many people blame parents for their children's behavior and naively offer advice that they are certain will "cure" ADHD. A woman at one of my workshops proclaimed with great irritation that these people usually live in The Land of the "Just." "If you would *just* make him use a planner," many parents of non-ADHD children maintain, "then you would know what his homework was, and you could make sure that he did it!" As a parent at one of my workshops said, "We would get him to use a planner if we could find one of the ninety-three planners that he's already lost!" I love Tammy Young's term for this type of recommendation: supermarket-generated advice.⁹ No one ever flippantly dispenses suggestions for dealing with a relative who suffers from schizophrenia. People with no training in medicine do not presume to know the ins and outs of diabetes. But with ADHD, everyone is an expert.

I am always amazed at the abject simplicity and complete lack of understanding of the people who give us unwanted advice. Here is one of my favorites: "If you would *just* make him do his homework right when he gets home, you wouldn't have a problem." The person who offers this nugget of wisdom obviously has neither encountered the adeptness of us ADHDers at inventing believable stories to explain a *lack* of homework, nor experienced our resilient aptitude for delay. I remember from Roman history that a consul named Fabius the Delayer kept the great Hannibal at bay through a series of delaying tactics. I think Fabius must have had ADHD. This military metaphor is appropriate because dealing with ADHDers can often seem like a protracted, unwinnable war of attrition.

JEEVES, WHERE ARE YOU?

I, along with many ADHDers, should have been born with my own manservant, someone to take care of the incidentals in life so that I could be free to indulge the frequent fancies of my creative mind. I love going off on a tangent, coming up with a new way of doing things, and crafting a fresh perspective on an old idea.

In many periods in history, people like me had a social structure that supported their creative endeavors. I watch those nineteenth-century British dramas on *Masterpiece Theatre*, and I long for the days when somebody like me, provided he had enormous amounts of land and money, could be wildly successful. Aristocrats each had a manservant or a lady-in-waiting. They didn't have to throw those elaborate parties and make preparations to go to war against rivals; their servants did all of that. Their job was to have all the big ideas. Practical skills were for "lesser" beings. Aristocrats would have been lost without their multiple attendants. Many of them didn't even dress or bathe themselves, for God's sake! Maybe they were all ADHD.

In nineteenth-century Europe, aristocrats made up 5 to 10 percent of the population, which strangely parallels the percentage of ADHD individuals in modern society. I suspect we're all aristocrats who are victims of a massive socioeconomic shift. If I had a manservant, a butler, a personal secretary, and a team of gardeners, I'm sure I would be worth millions and have the nicest-looking house on the block! Darn that French Revolution; it ruined my life.

I suspect that our aristocratic past accounts for the fact that many ADHDers are described as oppositional-defiant. For instance, if you agree with this paragraph, I will find a way to disagree, even though I wrote it. The way I look at it, we are hardwired to be in charge! If you took the average ADHD individual and set him or her up with a staff, things would be a lot different, and the right people would be in jail.

I do concede that the aristocrat metaphor only goes so far. Those long, formal dinners, for example, would have given many ADHDers trouble, not to mention the trials of tea time. Sipping tea from fine china and daintily handling the crumpets and cucumber sandwiches would have been quite a stretch. I really believe that if proper historical research were done, we'd find that ADHDers actually created the first food fight during an interminably long tea party at the palace of Versailles. In addition to our aversion to stiff culinary rituals, we would also have bristled at being ordered to marry someone "appropriate to our station in life." Just as many people during Britain's Victorian age felt oppressed by rigid social structures, ADHDers often find themselves at odds with modern social systems.

School is one system that runs counter to our intuition and impulses. I realized I was in an alien world on the very first day of school. Many small children actually like school for the first few years. I hated it from the very start. The expectations of school felt like shackles around my mind and body. As the years progressed, they nearly had to put shackles around me—Sister Raphael actually did duct-tape me to my chair on one occasion—just to get me to sit down.

I CAN'T HEAR YOU!

Every ADHD person will have stories like mine. Faced with powerful adults who seem arrayed against us, we become trench warfare specialists. We know how to hunker down, riding out the artillery barrage of loved ones nagging and yelling at us. And we even go on the offensive by sidetracking our "enemy" through eloquently crafted stories, excuses, and counter-accusations. "I don't have math to do tonight, because I was forced to stay in during recess and Mrs. Johnson made me do the homework," one of my coaching clients recently shared with his mother to rebuff her requests to start that evening's assignment. Doesn't this story sound authentic? I find myself particularly admiring how this ten-year-old boy hooked his mother into believing the lie: he linked his well-known tendency to misbehave, and thus to lose recess privileges, with the hard-to-accept fact that he had completed the math homework in school. Mom loved the fact that she wasn't going to have to spend another two hours ensuring that the work got done, like she did on most school nights. Her mental fatigue certainly played a role in her willingness to accept the story without proof. After learning the truth the next day, however, his mother seethed. "You got out of doing it yesterday," she laid into him, "but now you have twice as much. Why do you do this?"

When loved ones manage to successfully navigate through our half-truths and fabrications, we sometimes turn to blaming them for the work not getting done. "If you would stop bugging me, I would start my homework," Ryan told his father. "I just need a few minutes to relax and you won't even let me have that." The skill of ADHDers to turn the tables when it comes to nagging is admirable. And we do it with unconscious competence; this skill seems to reside in our hardwiring, but perhaps we develop it out of supreme necessity, as we are often the object of finger-pointing and faultfinding. Defending indefensible behavior and constant blame shifting make our lives and homes feel like battlegrounds. For many loved ones, being around an ADHDer feels like a war zone. Just like the experiences of most war veterans I've talked to, having an ADHD child or spouse is a case of not having a clue what it's like unless you've actually been there.

A CHANGED MAN

As I have worked more in-depth with kids, I have begun to appreciate firsthand the predicament of loved ones, and with my ADHD study groups and cyber recovery groups, I have often felt like I was in the middle of a war zone as well. I have increasingly found myself wrapped up in the same negative dynamics as the loved ones who bring their ADHDers to see me. I tend to take it personally when kids repeatedly fail to follow through on commitments they make to me: not filling out their planner every day, turning in work late, not exercising before attempting to study, etc. As I am sure many parents do, I began to wonder a while ago whether *I* was the problem and frequently spent my free time trying to devise ever more creative strategies and methods to get these kids to succeed. In some cases I was successful, but in many other cases I judged myself a failure. Like many with ADHD, I often chose to focus on my failures and shortcomings instead of my strengths. Old behaviors die hard. After about four years, I began to feel burned out.

In my early years as an ADHD coach, I plowed through the failures and kept on going. I had a vague notion that parents were bringing their kids to me in the spirit of abdicating their own responsibility. I realized quickly, though, that most parents desperately wanted to help their child, but unwittingly had participated in the negative dynamics that erected barriers between themselves and their child. The hurt feelings and intractable arguments prevented any strategies from being devised, let alone implemented. Blame flew back and forth, and both parents and children seemed more interested in winning the rhetorical high ground than uncovering workable solutions. I have been working with ADHDers for more than thirteen years now, and I must admit that only in the last six years have I been able to unravel the mystery of the relational games that ADHD people play.[10]

I saw that I was falling into the same role many parents find themselves in, and I decided to embark on a new path of self-discovery. I had some help from authors like Thom Hartmann, Daniel Amen, and Ned Hallowell. Hartmann helped me appreciate that ADHD represented an alternate way of viewing reality and had just as many benefits as drawbacks, in most cases. Hallowell led me to see that my mind sought constant and novel stimulation to increase overall brain activity, not because I was doing anything wrong. Amen switched on a light for me that illuminated the underpinnings of the ADHD tendency to create negative dynamics. These three authors have fundamentally altered my perspectives on ADHD as well as my own self-perceptions as an ADHDer. In the last six years, I have endeavored to bring their pieces of wisdom into my professional practice.

OPPOSITION

I've begun to understand the reasons why I often have no firm and fast opinions on politics, religion, or virtually any discussion topic—I take the opinion opposite to what others espouse. I have felt this sensation, an inner barometer, that discerns when a conversation is leaning too much to one side, and I single-handedly put it back into balance. I am a walking "yin-yang" machine in conversations. The impulse to do this remains strong, even now. If folks at my favorite coffee shop extol the virtues of Rush Limbaugh and his "precise political intuition," I automatically become a big fan of MSNBC and Rachel Maddow. If someone wistfully talks about the positives of the Clinton years in Washington, I immediately bring up *Whitewatergate* and Monica Lewinsky. I like to tell people that I am Libertarian so that I have legitimacy and ammunition to argue with both Republicans and Democrats. Why do I expend all this energy? Why do I waste my time in fruitless debates? Furthermore, why do these debates get my blood boiling? I have come to the inescapable conclusion that I feel more alive when I am being negative. Opposing something gives me more juice than supporting it.

We ADHDers create negative dynamics in many areas of our lives. Frequent arguments, broken promises, and insensitive interpersonal styles leave a trail of hurt feelings, disappointment, and bewilderment. ADHDers often exhibit incredible powers of precision in finding innovative methods to push other people's buttons. This ability, combined with the impact of years of negativity, often leaves the people in our lives feeling that we "do it on purpose." Parents, teachers, and spouses often take things personally, seeing us as bullies and instigators. Recent studies, however, strongly point to an underlying method to this seeming madness. Research demonstrates that negative information and stimulation weigh more heavily on the brain than do positive information and stimulation, thus creating more brain activity.[11] ADHD is, to a significant extent, a condition of decreased activity in several areas of the brain.[12] ADHDers must constantly bring in new stimulation to increase activity in the brain. Focusing singularly on one topic with sustained attention often decreases brain activity in ADHD folks, an assertion supported by numerous brain-imaging studies.[13] ADHD individuals create negative situations and dynamics as one unconscious way to increase cerebral activity.

Eric Berne, psychologist and author of *Games People Play*, posited that people who do not get their psychological needs met positively will unconsciously find negative ways to fulfill them.[14] Daniel Amen put his own twist on Berne's ideas when he coined the phrase, "games ADD people play." Whereas Berne focused on psychological needs, Amen concentrated on neurological ones. Essentially, we get juiced up by negative situations, which neurologically increases overall brain activity. Since ADHDers suffer from lower activity in certain cerebral regions, negativity can be regarded, in a manner of speaking, as a coping mechanism. It is well documented that untreated ADHDers have a significantly greater tendency to self-medicate through marijuana, cocaine, alcohol, and even behavioral addictions.[15] Many of us ADHDers use negativity in much the same way, to alter our brains. Just like illicit drugs, however, negativity in our lives has serious side effects, not only for the ADHDer, but for those around him or her as well. When I start seeing an ADHDer professionally, I often start our work together by dealing with the cumulative effects of years of negativity.

THE TASMANIAN DEVIL GOES TO SCHOOL

I am reminded of my first-grade teacher, Ms. Franklin. She discovered what would now be called ADHD traits in me not more than a month into the school year. She frequently kept me after school and made me skip recess to complete assignments that I just wasn't interested in. As I have gone through my old report cards from that year, it is clear that Ms. Franklin was most frustrated by what she saw as laziness, having the ability but choosing not to use it. She was a very conscientious teacher and she used, I am sure, virtually every imaginable trick to get me plugged in to school.

Noticing my interest in foreign languages, she brought in a French *Sesame Street* video and let me watch it with her. By the way, there is a difference: in the French version, Bert and Ernie are condescending and rude, and they have a strange taste for goose liver pâté. Observing my penchant for performance, Ms. Franklin invited me on several occasions to recite my favorite Dr. Seuss stories in front of the class. I still fondly recollect those sweet moments of showcasing my flare for drama. But I still wasn't going to do those mindless worksheets.

She tried a bit of humor when she described my rapid circular scribbling technique on worksheets as the "Tasmanian Devil coloring style." She did a Tasmanian Devil imitation in front of the class, and everybody, including me, laughed. I am sure she thought that this effort might evoke some shame in me and thus inspire me to modify my behavior. I loved being compared to that *Looney Tunes* madman. "Nobody beats Taz," I would gleefully shout on the playground. We boys even made a game out of it. Playing "Taz" involved a group of boys rapidly spinning, making physical contact, and trying to knock each other down. The game lasted only two weeks before Ms. Franklin forbade us from playing it, not only because she thought it was inappropriate but also because several boys were injured. She must have felt great frustration when for show-and-tell I brought in my Tasmanian Devil drinking glass and, in an attempt to demonstrate how "Taz" would drink, ended up spilling water on everyone in the front row.

When her efforts to "motivate" me failed, she called a meeting with my mother to discuss a very serious matter, as my mother tells the story. "Kevin shows no interest in coloring in objects on his worksheets," Ms. Franklin somberly informed my mother. "He just scribbles a few lines on each object and moves on; when he's finished, he socializes with the other children." They saw this as a bad thing. Obviously, Ms. Franklin had not read the biography of Pablo Picasso or seen any of his paintings, or those of Manet, Monet, Van Gogh, or Jackson Pollock. I could go on and on, but I've lost my train of thought. Ms. Franklin, however, did go on: "This is a serious problem, and I can't remember having had a student who was as much of a chatterbox as your son is."

> *ADHD individuals are frequently hands-on learners who demonstrate a need to use their hands as well as move their bodies. Because these needs are rarely met in school and at work, these folks tap their pencils, doodle, or create rhythms to "keep the beat." It is important that we view this hands-on orientation as a gift, not a liability. Doodlers could be enrolled in art classes and pencil tappers taught mechanics and woodworking. Others might excel at playing drums or other musical instruments.*

My mother was most concerned not because of what Ms. Franklin had told her, but rather by the other people who attended the meeting. Father Anderson, the church pastor, and Sister Nancy, the school's principal, both supported Ms. Franklin's claims, and the three of them urged my mother to action. An ardent and devoted Catholic, she could never have ignored the advice from men and women of the cloth. Sister Nancy gave my mother hope that a solution to my difficulties was right around the corner.

THE EXORCISM OF THE TASMANIAN DEVIL

We pulled into the church parking lot on a Wednesday evening. This perplexed me because, although church attendance was mandatory in our family, I had never been forced to go to church during the week, except for Christmas or, of course, Ash Wednesday. Like all Catholic-school ADHDers, I loved Ash Wednesday. I used to try to keep those ashes on my forehead for the whole week! But this was October, far from the beginning of Lent. "We're here to get you some help," my mother told me. "Sister Nancy said there are some people here who know how to help you behave in school." Unbeknownst to me, Sister Nancy had told her about something called a charismatic prayer group. The group met in our church basement once a week, and its members believed they had special access to the powers of the Holy Spirit. They believed that the gifts of the Holy Spirit had been lost and forgotten. Their mission was to bring those gifts back— one church basement at a time. My mother had no clue what she was getting us into, which is how she usually operated. She was desperate for me to succeed in school.

"I'm not going in there," I remember defiantly telling her. "Weird things happen when you go into basements with strangers." She said nothing and got out of the car. Before I knew what was happening, she grabbed my arm and pulled me toward the church. I heard singing and music, which piqued my curiosity, so I stopped resisting. We opened the door to the church hall, which, looking back, was a portal into a time the world had forgotten, and rightfully so.

A middle-aged woman with her arms outstretched was the first to catch my attention because of the strange string of unintelligible syllables she chanted: "Hadi hadi hadi hadi ahh . . . Hadi hadi hadi hadi ahh . . . Bam shalal . . . Hadi hadi hadi hadi ahh." Her refrain sounded like speech I had heard from the Arabic-speaking owners of our local party store or from the Cab Calloway records my stepfather played when he was drunk . . . "hidey, hidey, hidey, ho." I wasn't sure whether they were religious or members of the Scatman Crothers Fan Club. "She sounds like the Abrahams at the party store," I told my mother. She shushed me and shot me a very nasty look. I knew I had better be quiet.

I learned later that these people believed they were "speaking in tongues," the language of the Holy Spirit. For those who "received" this gift, the Holy Spirit, they believed, would take over their speech and every syllable out of their mouths would come from God. The problem was that when they were asked, they could never tell you what they had just said. They would stare blankly, as though I had just spoken to them in a foreign tongue, then jump up and down for joy and shout, "Praise you, Jesus! Praise you, Lord!"

My mother, a very traditional Catholic, ushered me to the back of the room, where we sat silently. She was quite uncomfortable. Her discomfort, much to my chagrin, was not enough for her to engineer an escape from this madness. The elders of our church had sent us to that basement, and by God, we were staying. Besides, I think she was digging the tunes.

The prayer meeting lasted more than an hour and consisted of joyous hymns followed by thunderous explosions of speaking in tongues. When the "tongues" died down, the guitarist and singers would start another song: "Praise him, praise him/Praise him in the morning, praise him at the noontime/Praise him, praise him/Praise him when the sun goes down." My mother, a long-time member of the choir, did not join in these hymns of praise. The excitement of the event made it easier for me to sit for an hour. There was never a dull moment. I wish you could randomly jump up and down and shout for joy in school. I would have been an academic star!

After the meeting, Al, the man in charge of this mayhem, approached my mother. He knew, without asking, who we both were and why we had come. "I'd like to take both of you to the prayer room," he sternly said. *The prayer room?* I wondered to myself. *This is bad.* The three of us and the rest of the prayer team went to a small room, where I was led to a worn-out, powder-blue La-Z-Boy recliner. I was beginning to wonder if I was going to be saved or become one of those kids you see on the side of a milk carton. Al started right in, as my mother dutifully stood by my side. He put his right hand on my head and attempted to call on the Almighty to intervene in my predicament. Al began what he called his intercessory incantation: "Lord, you have blessed this boy with great genius," which was news to me. The other five members of the prayer team followed Al's words in unison, "Praise God." As he spoke, some would randomly go off speaking in tongues. Al continued, "You have given him great energy, too, Lord." I couldn't argue with him there. "Sometimes, people don't have enough energy, Lord, and that's when you step in and multiply, like you did with the loaves and the fishes. But sometimes, Lord, other people have too much, and we ask you to help this boy with too much energy so that he can channel it and magnify your name." With that line, the prayer team went off on a several-minute, speaking-in-tongues frenzy. Al's hot and sweaty hand was on my head the whole time and the room smelled of body odor. Finally, they all put their sweaty hands on me and left them there for what seemed an eternity. After what I think must have been four or five minutes, Al slowly and deliberately removed his hand, and the others followed his lead. Al declared to my mother, "God has told me he has healed this boy. His troubles are over."

I actually was healed. I knew I never wanted that many stinky, sweaty hands on me ever again, at least not until I was nineteen or twenty. Amazingly, I had fewer difficulties in school for a while after that, even though La-Z-Boys still scare me. I never wanted to go back to that prayer room.

LESSONS LEARNED

I am reminded of the book *All I Really Need to Know I Learned in Kindergarten*. For me, it was first grade. I learned that I had such *serious problems* that God almighty was the only one who could offer me any assistance. I learned that my way of being in the world was not adequate, and I have been trying to break free from that lesson ever since. A good deal of my personal growth work has involved navigating through this negative belief pattern, and I think I have finally been making some progress. It is not so much that I have changed, but that I have learned to live with my true nature.

School was not structured for me. Very early on, I, like many ADHDers, had an impulse to resist. Many of us are natural rebels. "Hey, I've got an idea: let's board that British ship and throw all the tea in the water." You think maybe the Boston Tea Party had a few ADHD participants? Events in the first few years of school showed me that I needed to hide some parts of myself and keep my burgeoning rebellious nature in check. It was so hard, especially in a strict Catholic school.

I remember once in second grade, my class was in the church with the dreaded Sister Raphael. Not only did we have to contend with her in school, but she also had the habit of walking through the neighborhood, always on the lookout for sinners. On many occasions I would be outside playing with my friends and see her scowling by. Catching sight of her always ruined whatever we were doing. When I watched *The Empire Strikes Back* and saw the Emperor on the big screen for the first time, I was sure George Lucas had based that character on her. "Ralph," as she was known by students, had a pushed-in face with cavernous wrinkles. Combined with a quick temper and a heavy Scottish brogue, she scared the living daylights out of all of us, but not enough to get me to conform.

While practicing for our First Communion ceremony that day in second grade, we processed in a single-file line up to the altar. All the kids walked on the right side of the lectern on their way to the altar, even though no one had specifically told them to do that. I decided, absent explicit instructions, to walk around to the left and then quickly rejoin the line. "What in God's name do you think you're doing?" she yelled, as terror vibrated inside me. "Get over here now!" The spanking I received made it hard to sit down for a few days. "But nobody told us we couldn't go that way," I protested, which only led to further spanking and scolding. The playful impulse of a bored little boy was treated as blasphemy. What I learned was to make sure that my fun took place as far away from certain adults as possible. I learned to conceal my playful and mischievous nature and, like many Catholic boys and girls of my generation, how to lie. But in spite of being resilient and rebellious, I took on some bad messages. Something about me was just not acceptable.

Again, I have not really changed much since those early years. I have, however, worked to eliminate those highly toxic messages that were thrust upon me. I have learned to celebrate my strengths and get support for my weaknesses. My first-grade and second-grade behavior has persisted well into adulthood, which is why I pay professionals to paint my house (adult coloring), hire an accountant to do my taxes (which reminds me of the mindless worksheets from grade school), and have a maid service clean for me—I would have won the "Messy Desk Award" every year in school, hands down! Just like in first grade, I am an extraordinarily social being, and this is exactly what allows me to tune in to ADHD children and adults and help them develop strategies to live in the world in a way that is congruent with their deeper selves.

When a person, like me and other ADHD individuals, doesn't fit within the system, the individual is said to be disordered, troubled, or abnormal. Biological research strongly suggests that factors inside the ADHD individual correlate with the "disordered" behavior,[16] but the narrow learning paradigms of our society certainly play a significant role. The limitations of our academic systems have not been given careful treatment by the mental health and academic communities. I have not yet figured out a way to shift the educational and social paradigms on a grand scale, so I have spent my energies trying to help ADHD individuals develop strategies to cope in society.

LIGHTENING UP

I made many serious mistakes when I first started offering workshops to help parents lighten up. I went quickly for the jugular, trying to get parents to see the error of their ways, so they could choose new behaviors that would instantly benefit them and their children. I wanted to lead them out of negativity and into the promised land of better relationships, so they could help their children succeed instead of alienating them. The only problem with this model was that the parents revolted. "You'd be negative, too, if you had to live with my son," one mother blasted me. "You don't know what I've been through." Despite the fact that parents had come to the workshop to "lighten up," many of them were not ready. After many such encounters, I came to believe that their intransigence derived from the perception that I was diminishing what they had gone through. I determined that a frontal assault was not going to work.

Somewhat frustrated, I decided to try different approaches. One that worked exceedingly well was designed to honor their experiences before offering them the opportunity to change. Parents sat down, and I started by explaining my prior errors. When I told them that "other parents had revolted," they all laughed. "I don't want a revolt on my hands today," I told them, "so I am handing out note cards for you to write down your three best stories of ADHD madness." I further explained that they should include the most outrageous things their child had done and not write their names on the cards. After four or five minutes, they passed the note cards to the front and I started reading them off.

As I read aloud one painful episode after another, parents identified with each other's stories. At first, they knowingly nodded, communicating that they had been there too. They slowly relaxed. To my surprise, they started laughing after a few minutes. The support in the room allowed them to laugh at their kids' behavior and with each other. The commonalities of their stories allowed them to lighten up.

This process honored their suffering, so that they could begin to move past it. I was astounded that my first impulses on how to help parents lighten up were totally wrong. To get them to laugh at their predicament, I had to first lead them through their pain. The method that finally worked was the exact opposite of what I originally had in mind. That piece of wisdom more than any other has served me faithfully these last several years.

Be Nice to Teachers

Teachers receive an education that generally prepares them well to meet the needs of the majority of students. Most do not, however, receive much training to prepare them for the challenges of having an ADHD student in the classroom. We have to be careful to not vilify teachers. In dealing with the teachers of my ADHD students, I have generally found compassion and support, but these dedicated folks often have a load of 150 students. With strained budgets, the training and in-services that could give teachers the tools and information they need about ADHD have been gravely curtailed. If you are approaching the teachers of your ADHD loved one, please go into the situation with understanding and empathy for the predicament of teachers. You could also follow the advice of Sherry Miller, whose ADHD son also has some serious processing issues: take bagels, donuts, brownies, and coffee to every meeting. The teachers are always glad to see her!

Many of the traits that caused me to have friction with the school system and other social venues are exactly the same traits that make me funny and fun to be around. When I taught school, Brian, one of my brightest students, said that having me as a teacher was like being taught by Kramer from the *Seinfeld* show: "You just never know what's going to happen from one moment to the next. I never want to miss your class, Kevin [students and teachers were on a first-name basis at The Roeper School]. I'd be too afraid I'd miss something."

I had always longed to be just like everybody else, but here was a student telling me I was different and that he wouldn't have had it any other way. My four years at The Roeper School made me see what should have been obvious all along: I make people laugh. People are never bored around me. I have provided comic relief to those around me in countless monotonous situations, and, at the very least, have given dull people something to talk about. Most of my unique gifts and talents, however, were not honored by the institution in which I physically used to spend roughly 40 percent of my waking hours. I have spent the last sixteen years working through issues surrounding that fact. It is my hope to save as many people as I can from the long and harried journey I have endured.

ALWAYS A DISORDER?

Some researchers advocate for reframing ADHD as an "atypical" way of processing along one or more "continua." This view argues for a perspective that sees ADHD as simply a condition diagnosed by an extreme presentation of traits that, in less extreme forms, would be useful and fall into the normal range:

> When the continuous nature of ADHD, as a trait, is recognized, the categorical distinction of "affected" versus "unaffected" will become less important because the underlying liability does not match this clinical distinction. Second, the continua underlying ADHD may be distinguished from the "disorder" in that the trait continua may be impairing in some environmental contexts and less impairing or even advantageous in others.[17]

From a personality perspective, the "continua" that under-lie ADHD can be easily ascertained. Some people, for example, are spontaneous by nature. An extreme form of spontaneity is impulsivity, an important diagnostic criterion in ADHD. Some people are naturally flexible and adaptable,[18] but in extreme cases these traits could show up as a short attention span and lack of interest in completing the details of a task, traits also associated with ADHD. ADHDers often present with the "negative" extremes of positive and useful traits. Taking into account the ADHD way of viewing the world would likely help to diminish the negatives and bring out more positives, as well as act as a fail-safe for inaccurate and inappropriate ADHD diagnoses. So many examples exist of ADHDers who had trouble in school but then went on to lead fulfilling and successful lives.

A growing number of professionals believe that it is useful to view ADHD as a set of predispositions for experiencing the world. Professionals of this mindset urge others to consider a strengths-based approach, one that takes into account the unique positive traits that ADHD often imparts. ADHD individuals, according to this perspective, often perform well in jobs requiring a lot of action, high intensity, creativity, and entrepreneurship.[19] Since these aptitudes are not usually encouraged or recognized in the classroom, students so predisposed often end up feeling academically inadequate and suffer from self-esteem issues, in addition to being referred for psychological testing. But almost every ADHDer remembers a teacher whose style was perfect and in whose class the student achieved a high level of performance. I went to Catholic Central High School outside of Detroit, Michigan, and in ninth grade, I had several such teachers.

FULL-CONTACT ACADEMICS

Many teachers still used corporal punishment at that school, although I have to say that it was not administered with brutality or malice. There was almost a playful roughhousing aspect to it, which many boys need. The corporal aspect of classroom management was one that still seemed particularly insidious to me, given my prior family experiences. I had, after all, seen my siblings get beaten by my stepfather, but I had avoided their fate. I intended to keep my *winning streak* going. When I got home from school, those images helped motivate me to do my homework. The threat of repercussions propelled me into academic stardom.

Despite the excesses of some of the teachers at my high school, I must admit that I felt more alive there than ever before. I began to feel the depths of my intellectual power for the first time in my life. I became certain that I was a highly intelligent person. Confusion on this matter began to evaporate. Had I gone to a regular public high school, I would have continued along the same path of academic embezzlement that had worked for me for more than eight years.

I am not condoning everything that went on in high school, but I am saying that there were things about it that worked for me. Ultimately, I felt empowered by my teachers and later I wondered how we could inject some more intensity into high schools—without corporal punishment—so that other ADHD young people could have that same type of opportunity to use their brains.

I didn't have to wait long for my opportunity, because my first dose of that intensity came on the second day of ninth grade in Algebra One class with Father Baumeister. It should have been called "Full Contact Algebra." I'm convinced that he developed his gruff-voiced, no-nonsense teaching style from the military persona of General George Patton. He regularly pummeled boys in the chest, barked out orders, and belligerently planted himself behind boys who were struggling to do math problems at the board. I was shocked after the first day of class, but somehow I felt strangely activated. I went around school that day with a hypervigilance and focus that I had never before experienced. My mind was engaged, and I paid attention in each and every Algebra One class as though my life depended on it, because I was pretty sure that it did.

I found no humor the day one unfortunate boy made a simple mistake. He was at the board working a problem and mixed up the sine and cosine ratios. Baumeister rushed over to where the young man was working, cocked his hand back, and walloped him hard across the chest. The boy flew back into the third row of desks. "You're yellow!" Baumeister barked. "You're not going to live to see the tenth grade if you can't keep simple information straight." After that, he read out the next problem he wanted the class to solve, as though nothing unusual had happened.

I asked my mother, much to her amazement, to take me in early on the fourth day of school so I could meet with Father Baumeister. There were a few problems I was unsure about, and I wanted to make sure that they were all correct. I had done them all, of course, but I left nothing to chance. One incorrect problem could send Baumeister into a rage, and I might have been the target. Everyone was a dumb Irishman, or a dumb Frenchman, and one kid—who I think was of German descent—had a name that sounded Chinese to Baumeister's ears. That boy was called "chink" for the remainder of the year. I still struggle with the paradox of it all: this man was verbally and physically abusive, prone to rage, and yet I credit him with a strong role in my academic salvation. I went back a few years ago and listened from the hall to one of his classes. I was filled with both disgust and gratitude.

BRAIN AFIRE

My brain was on fire that first year, thanks to Father Baumeister. I was a whirling dervish of activity because, in my mind, my academic success was necessary to avoid a classic, Catholic-priest beat-down. For me, the school was an academic proving ground. As I look back, what amazes me is that, whereas no teacher in my first eight years of school had inspired me, almost all of my ninth-grade teachers did. Some I feared, while I craved the approval of others. The intensity propelled me.

The inability of the "normal" classroom environment to positively engage ADHDers, however, can lead those with ADHD to exhibit negative behaviors in a vain attempt to engage with the teacher. Teachers almost always perceive such negative behavior as reflecting a problem within the student, not within their own pedagogical and interpersonal approaches.

Several learning-style models have demonstrated that students of all shapes and sizes have greater success in the classroom environment when their psychological needs are met and when information is communicated in a way that fits with their perceptual preferences and preferred channels of communication.[20] One 2002 study found that ADHD children perform much better with relatively low levels of light and when they have opportunities for frequent breaks.[21] It was also found that ADHD children need more encouragement from parents and teachers to function optimally, which relates to the fact that ADHD individuals are usually extrinsically motivated. Pedagogical flexibility has the potential to improve outcomes for all students, but especially those with ADHD.

A strengths-based model of ADHD views lack of success in the classroom as deriving, at least in part, from the fact that ADHD students learn differently and do not receive adequate accommodation for their differences. They, like all individuals, have unique perceptual preferences for taking in information, communicating with others, and interacting with the world around them.[22] Such preferences in ADHD people have, however, been viewed almost completely through the "disorder" lens. Scant attention has been given to considering ADHD as simply a way of being, with its own advantages and disadvantages. As a result, very few studies have examined the role the environment plays in producing the negative behaviors that usually lead to an ADHD diagnosis, although family influences have been shown to affect the development of personality and adjustment disorders in ADHD individuals.[23]

School is viewed as a necessary rite of passage, yet for many ADHDers the experience is so counter to their natural predispositions that it becomes a downright hindrance to happiness. Although I have a different perspective and great appreciation for my uniqueness now, grade school ground me down. I did not want to "need" intercessory prayer, so like many a gifted ADHDer, I developed elaborate deceptions to help me maintain a facade of normalcy.

Underneath many of the "side effects" of ADHD, you will often find useful coping skills that can, under the right guidance and mentoring, be harnessed. If you want to help an ADHDer, or his or her loved ones, the way to go about it is usually contrary to your knee-jerk reactions.

CHAPTER 3

DO THE OPPOSITE

"Stick . . . with the opposite."
Elaine Benes, character from *Seinfeld*

NO COMMON SENSE

Trying to help an ADHDer create lasting change can be a thankless task, if not an exercise in futility. Difficulty with follow-through is, after all, one of the most common characteristics of the condition. The first mistake most people make is thinking ADHD folks are just like them. If ADHDers could conform to accepted behavioral standards, armchair wisdom holds, their troubles would be over. Many of the choices we ADHDers make seem counter to logic and reason, and why we don't make simple changes in our lives continually confounds those close to us. ADHDers do not readily accept suggestions from those closest to them, those who most certainly have their best interests at heart. Often, the more they try to help the ADHDer, the more they succeed in pushing that person away.

People start with the best of intentions, but they fail to appreciate that effective approaches to help ADHDers often defy intuition. When parents and spouses come to see me, and when I talk to groups of teachers and therapists, I try to communicate that, in many ways, we ADHDers inhabit a different universe. Anyone who sincerely wants to help and understand us must be willing to let go of preconceptions and perhaps even common sense.

When I ponder the gulf between ADHDers and the rest of humankind, I am reminded of John Gray's book *Men Are from Mars, Women Are from Venus*. Gray conceptualizes the differences between male and female modes of thinking and feeling in terms of alignment with planets and thus with their corresponding Roman deities. Although I do not completely agree with Gray's concept, I do think the metaphor is useful. So what gods and planets should we associate with ADHDers? We inhabit a precarious position in the world, so I am not sure we even have our own planet. It may feel to some that we hail from another galaxy. For us, the demands of school and society can make us feel that going to another galaxy would be an improvement.

AN ADHD MYTHOLOGY

It takes strong powers of persuasion for me to convince ADHD folks that their condition has as many positives as it does negatives. Such an assertion flies in the face of the panoply of negative pronouncements they have endured, not to mention the consensus of the scientific community! Growing up in a world that constantly points out one's flaws makes it difficult to uncover one's gifts and potential.

I keep an eye out for success stories and have a folder in which I file articles about innovative ADHD individuals. I bring up noteworthy ADHDers like David Neeleman, the founder of JetBlue Airways, whose example shows how ADHD folks often excel as entrepreneurs.[1] I go over my thesis that Oskar Schindler, made famous in Spielberg's film *Schindler's List*, had ADHD and needed the intensity of a world at war to bring out his inner genius and compassion. Many ADHDers do function well in intensity and crisis. Just as many have harped on them about their flaws and failures, I harp on my clients about their talents and future possibilities.

Constantly on the lookout for stories that highlight ADHD

success, I started searching through Greek myths. I quickly noticed kindred spirits who embodied qualities that would surely resonate with many an ADHDer. To start with, we are adventurers, often ill at ease with domesticity. The world's mythologies are replete with such individuals. Like Jason setting off to find the Golden Fleece and Theseus battling the Minotaur, we embrace danger and long to test our powers in some grand undertaking. Those of us who might be called daydreamers achieve this spirit of adventure through fantasy and vivid journeys of the mind. Like Daedalus and Icarus in the Labyrinth, life for us often feels like a prison that we long to flee. We have lofty ideas for escape, but like Icarus, we often get too close to the sun and quickly burn out. Life is a struggle.

As Atlas fought with the chief god Zeus, so we often find ourselves in trouble with authority figures and their uncompromising codes of behavior. In the same way that Atlas was condemned to hold up the sky to atone for his transgressions, those in authority over us often impose punishments to dissuade us from our "waywardness." I remember one nun at my Catholic grade school telling me that I was being punished to help me "follow God's plan." If sitting still, keeping my mouth shut, and completing rote worksheet after rote worksheet were key elements of God's plan, I was destined to be a heretic.

Artemis, Greek goddess of the hunt, is one deity, however, whose plan I think I could actually follow and one whom most ADHDers should surely venerate. Artemis draws her power from the wilds of nature; those who deal with us, of course, brand us as forces of nature, calling us tornadoes or perhaps even Tasmanian Devils. Furthermore, many of us ADHDers seem quite at home in the natural world, a fact confirmed by a recent scientific study. Researchers at the University of Illinois found that ADHD children demonstrated greater attention after a twenty-minute walk in a forest than after a similar walk in a downtown area or residential neighborhood.[2] Scientists noted that ADHD children had a much easier time completing homework and studying after these nature walks.

Thom Hartmann has also written about the ADHD fondness for nature. He calls us hunters, those rare folks who constantly scan the environment (a trait negatively labeled as distractibility) and are able to go on the chase at a moment's notice (negatively labeled as impulsivity).[3] When you walk through the woods with one of us ADHDers, you'll probably notice that we are often the first ones to spot the deer or bird in the distance. We love being outside, and we naturally and constantly shift our attention to ascertain what is going on around us.

Somewhere among the stars, Artemis, the nature-affirming goddess of the hunt, has her own planet, a place where the ADHD mindset is the norm. Journey now to that planet with me. The rules there are different.

ADHD SCHOOLS

Schools on the planet Artemis encourage discovery and exploration. The thirteen-year-old students of one school are studying grammar this week and they've just been sent out with tape recorders and paper to take notes on how people at the local market speak. When they return from their fieldwork at the market, they will listen to the different speech patterns and word usages they recorded and will then engage in a discussion about grammatical irregularities and anomalies. A few of the children, adept at imitation, will entertain the others with ad-lib renditions of some of the more colorful characters they encountered. Some children will eventually grow bored with the discussion, of course, and it is likely that the teacher will interrupt the grammatical discourse with ten to fifteen minutes of intense exercise. She finds that this method works especially well with adolescents.

As we move to another classroom, the students are learning about planetary motion. They are arrayed in the formation of their solar system. The teacher finds that the students learn better with a hands-on, interactive approach. She is not only teaching science but also instructing students to pay attention to details; each student, for example, must move in an orbital pattern at the relative speed of the planet she or he is embodying. Such a teaching method requires students to work in a group as well as alone. Each student is given fifteen minutes to find out the speed at which his or her respective planet revolves around the central star and also to research any interesting facts. The teacher has an audible clock ticking to help create an environment of intensity.

Knowing the value of intensity in the learning environment, she teaches about gravity and the laws of planetary motion by having students line up in two columns, one side being "planets" and the other side "moons." "Now lock hands and pull," she tells them, "until you reach a stable position. That's what gravity does. The planet holds its moon in place, but as you can feel, the moon pulls on the planet too." One student asks, "Is that how we get tides?" In the front of the room, one very strong boy can't help but pull his "moon" all the way across. Rather than scold him, the teacher says, "This is what happens with a black hole. Its gravity is so strong that it pulls in all other objects." She uses a boy's seemingly inappropriate behavior as an opportunity to teach and gives the students a powerful image to illustrate a scientific concept, one that will now likely stick in their minds.

The history teacher is quite fond of military matters, and rather than talking about famous military engagements, he takes his class outside to illustrate battles on the playground. He teaches about military formations, strategies, and tactics. Students march, attack, and retreat. The details of those battles live in the muscle memory of the students. They will remember those lessons for years to come.

TACTICS NEVER KEEP PACE WITH TECHNOLOGY

These teaching methods play to the strengths of ADHD. The teachers find ways to use these strengths to great effect. Many parents and teachers, however, expend great energy trying to help ADHD folks, with seemingly little effect. "I have tried everything with my son," a father named Roger told me, "but the impact I've had is pretty much negligible. He is an impregnable fortress of resistance." Although Roger had devoted almost all of his free time to helping his son succeed in school, the grades of the fourteen-year-old hovered close to failing. "I yell at him and take things away," Roger said, "but it doesn't do any good and makes the house seem like a war zone." Like most generals in war zones throughout history, Roger had decided on a frontal assault with his son. This almost never works with an ADHDer.

I am reminded of the Civil War and World War I. Scholars have attributed the high rate of casualties in both conflicts to the fact that although weapons had changed drastically, tactics had not. With the deadly accuracy of the rifled musket in the Civil War, massing troops and charging enemy positions became practically the same as suicide. The experience and training of the commanders, however, taught them to pursue and hold fast to the assault techniques that would ultimately lead to the slaughter of their soldiers. They did not adapt. Similarly, in World War I, the widespread use of the machine gun and fortified entrenchments made frontal assaults even more prone to failure, killing or permanently scarring millions of young men in Europe. Essentially, the tactics had not kept pace with the technology. Openness to new strategies by the commanding generals could have saved millions of lives. Similarly, we know more about ADHD than ever before, but many of us have not changed tactics.

I now ask you, the reader, to be a critically thinking battlefield commander. Look at the conflicts and conversations you have on a daily or weekly basis with the ADHDer in your life and notice how you respond. Before you read on, take a little time and honestly evaluate how you react to your ADHDer and what tangible benefits you see from those reactions.

Take out a piece of paper and make three columns. In the left column, write "Troubling Behaviors." In the middle, write "My Responses." And in the right column, write "Does It Work?" The following is an excerpt from a behavioral journal that was done by the father of one of my clients:

Troubling Behaviors	My Responses	Does It Work?
Missing assignments	Taking away computer, video games. Yelling, criticizing.	No. He sneaks to get access. If he does turn in assignments, it does not last.
Lying	Lots of yelling. I take it personally and get really mad at him.	Not in the least. He keeps lying. He has become better at deception.
Chores not done	I rescind his allowance and often get really mad.	Only if he wants money or has an IMMEDIATE reward of something he wants.
Does not take meds	I blow my stack and lecture him repeatedly.	For a while, but he still "forgets" to take them.

This father really wanted to change. I told him that the most important thing at the beginning was to be radically honest about how he was reacting. I also asked him to tape-record himself. "When I listened to the tapes of myself," he said, "I cringed, because I was like a broken record, not to mention the fact that I sounded an awful lot like my father when he raged at me." This father first got honest with himself about what he was doing. The tape recording was powerful because he could listen to it when he was calm and objective. "If I were him," the man said, "I would tune out too. I don't know how I'm going to change how I treat him, but I do know I'm going to stop what I've been doing." Insanity has often been described as doing the same thing over and over and expecting a different result. By changing our approach, we achieve a different result.

SCOLDING: A SUCCESSFUL STRATEGY?

Many parents of ADHDers feel that their lives are similar to that of the character played by Bill Murray in the movie *Groundhog Day*. The same patterns play out in a predictable cycle that parents and children never seem to move beyond. A ray of hope at the beginning of the school year for finally doing well, for example, is dashed with the arrival of progress reports in mid-October. What started off as a promising academic trajectory has deteriorated into a repeat of lying, missing assignments, and receiving low grades. Frustrated, parents revert to the same litany of rhetorical questions:

- "Can't you just turn in your assignments?"

- "Don't you know that how you do in school is how you'll do in life?"

- "Haven't you learned your lesson that when you don't write it down, it doesn't get done?"

- "Don't you get it yet that when you put things off, they never happen?"

- "How many times do I have to tell you that you can't just wait until the night before?"

When I am not at my best, I must admit that I, too, fall into this pattern with my students and coaching clients. When I realize such personal lapses go against my own advice, I hate myself for a few minutes, because it is just so hard to bear, realizing that I have been doing the same things to ADHDers for which I criticize other people.

Those who deal with ADHDers need to understand the situation from our perspective in order to gauge the efficacy of their reactions. Having been repeatedly lambasted with questions that arise out of frustration with us, we learn over time to tune out, and some in our ranks go on the offensive when confrontation is unavoidable. Once we develop the ability to put up our walls of defense, most cajoling and criticisms are wasted effort. We have a knack for continuing to play video games, watch TV, or surf the Internet, while at the same time our loved ones yell and scream at us. Rapidly shifting attention does have its benefits! This situation has prompted many a teacher, parent, or spouse to proclaim, "I feel like I'm wasting my breath on you!"

AVOIDANCE IN ACTION

Yes, we seemingly fail to live up to our potential, but sometimes we just cannot take any more criticism. Before my mind was awakened in ninth grade, I had been constantly reminded of my failures by my eighth-grade teacher, Mrs. Mulholland. She was a worn-out, putrid-breathed, blue-haired, sixty-something veteran of the classroom who hammered me with a steady battery of insults. She couldn't believe that I got accepted into the elite Catholic high school I was headed for. Mrs. Mulholland was pretty sure that I wouldn't be able to handle the academic load. I was sure I could, because I had been handling the load she'd been dishing out the whole of eighth grade. "That's a college prep school," she snarled, "and I'm not sure that you're college material." If nothing else, she was inspirational. She had "taught" (notice that word is in quotes) all of my siblings, whose failures she never tired of sharing. "Your sister Wendy never shut up either," she told me. "Didn't I hear she got kicked out of Our Lady of Perpetual Help?" I not only hated Mrs. Mulholland (or Mulch, as we *affectionately* referred to her), but I saw annoying her as an act of family honor.

Her classes left me mentally exhausted. I played sick more that year than I ever had in my life. And that's really saying something, because I had malingering down to a science. The biting drone of Mulch's lectures inspired me to go to greater heights. The sheer number of absences I had racked up made it hard to stay under the radar, necessitating a high level of creativity to continue those sweet days of sleeping in, TV reruns, and luxurious lounging. I would prepare my mother in advance so that on the day I actually wanted to miss school, she was well primed to believe my story:

> **Monday morning:** "Mom, I don't feel good, but I have to go to school because we're having a test." (There probably was no test.)
> **Monday after school:** "Mom, I still don't feel good. I'm going to go to my room and lie down." (My room was down-

stairs, where I could hang out and have fun with her being none the wiser.)

Tuesday morning: "Mom, I feel worse. Do you think I should go again?"

This tactic resulted in my mother suggesting that I stay home on Tuesday! "The stress of that school is really bringing you down," she said as she stroked my hair. "It'll be great next year when you're out of there, dear." For a while, she thought that my frequent illnesses resulted from the stress of Mulch's class, but even my trusting mother started to get suspicious. I resorted to tactics of ever-increasing complexity. I made mixtures of tomato soup and Aim toothpaste that I slowly poured into the toilet after I made a gut-curdling sound to pretend I was vomiting. I left my "handiwork" in the bowl in case she wanted to see, which she actually did on one occasion. That one almost backfired. After seeing the reddish-green sludge, she almost rushed me to the hospital. "You must have a bleeding ulcer!" she screeched. "Is that your kidney in there?"

Fevers were easier to feign. I would hold a heating pad on my forehead to simulate having a high temperature. This became standard procedure. I still don't understand why my mother never actually took my temperature with a thermometer. With the disorganization of our house, she probably couldn't find one. The cherry on top of this technique was to open the bathroom window—in the middle of winter—and hang my head out for a minute or so, which turned my face beet red. Sometimes, my mother would still make me go to school.

If all else failed, I would pull out the granddaddy of them all: the "diarrhea excuse." That one could always be counted on to carry the day. It amazes me to this day that no one ever questions the diarrhea excuse. Then again, who really wants to check? You have to use it sparingly, but as long as you do that, it's the old, reliable fail-safe of excuses. If you're a real pro like me, you sometimes act out doubling over, and while in the middle of a sentence, stop and quickly run to the bathroom again.

My excessive excuse-making behaviors came from having a teacher I thought was out to get me. In no way was Mulch equipped to handle the spastic shenanigans of adolescent males. She would have been great at an all-girls school. She hated all the boys, though, especially me. She was a gnarly nemesis, a force of nature. She was less a human being and more a mythological monster. The strength of her negative opinions cut deeply, even though I tried to put on a tough face. As much as I blew her off, she had an impact on me. I desperately wanted to prove her wrong. As I started ninth grade, I thought about her all the time. She was my inspiration. I don't know if she ever knew how much of a role she played in my transformation. I hated her . . . and my hatred made me powerful.

NEED YOUR BUTTONS PUSHED?

I took every opportunity to irritate Mulch. When her back was turned, I bombarded her with spit balls, left nasty anonymous notes on her desk, and took every opportunity to be a smart aleck. I can't imagine how she continued to teach someone who behaved as I had toward her, but she kept going. She never uttered a kind or affirming word in my direction, but I made sure to rarely exhibit behavior that would have elicited such responses. It was a dance of dysfunction that we were both caught in.

We ADHDers are masters at pushing people's buttons. Someone will yell at us for doing something. We profusely apologize or lie. Then, when the person's back is turned for a minute, we repeat the same exact behavior for which we have just been scolded. This may feel to the person as if the ADHDer has just elevated a giant middle finger in his or her direction. It seems as though we don't care and we want to "piss the other person off." So we get yelled at some more, with a little righteous indignation and martyrdom added for good measure. At the risk of sounding like a broken record, I must point out again our unmatched consistency in repeating the same behavior. Most people without ADHD would agree that the methods for motivating us to change do not often achieve their intended results, at the very least. And they often produce even more aggravating behavior. This was all true in my relationship with Mrs. Mulholland.

> *Working memory is the ability to "hold in" information that will be used in later responses and actions.[4] Working memory is impaired in ADHD.[5] If doing my homework is interrupted by a text message from a friend, an impaired working memory means that I may forget to go back and finish. It is the circuitry in the ADHD brain, and not a choice by ADHDers, that accounts for this deficit![6]*

So maybe it's time for you to change some of your strategies, to watch your reactions, and to choose your responses more carefully. Remember, we ADHDers thrive on negativity as a dysfunctional method to create activity in the brain. Your negative reactions are simply cannon fodder for us; we secretly love it! If you stopped reacting negatively, we would be at a great loss. In fact, once you start stepping out of the negative patterns, our efforts to get you to react will invariably increase.[7] We have, after all, become accustomed to turning on our brains through negativity, and when you take that away from us, we will have to find other methods. We rarely give up easily. We are hardy combatants!

You have probably recognized that you react quickly, perhaps even unconsciously, to the ADHDer in your life. I bet it almost feels as though you have no choice in the matter, that you must react, since such behavior has to be met with disapproval to "teach them a lesson." When it comes to ADHD children, we remember the biblical adage "Spare the rod; spoil the child." If any children deserve the rod, ADHDers certainly must. I think many parents would consider themselves remiss if they didn't administer harsh punishments to their ADHD child. I am going to offer you a radical recommendation: let go of all your assumptions and all your reactions to the ADHDer in your life.

Consider suspending them temporarily to make room for new ones.

You might find that a good many of the responses that work with an ADHDer are actually opposite and contrary to intuition and common sense. A great irony is that the recommendations I am about to make were inspired by an episode of the TV show *Seinfeld*. The character of George Costanza constantly laments that nothing in his life has worked out. Like George, I have bemoaned the lack of success in certain areas of my life, but I haven't associated it with my actions and inactions. It amazes me how long it sometimes takes me to realize my lack of progress is directly related to my stubborn behavior. I often look at the world and expect it to change to accommodate me. In an episode called "The Opposite," George experiences a stunning personal revelation that temporarily changes his behavior and then leads, for a time, to success in dating and his career:[8]

> **George:** It became very clear to me sitting out there today that every decision I've ever made in my entire life has been wrong. My life is the opposite of everything I want it to be. Every instinct I have . . . it's all been wrong.

This epiphany leads George to try a new method of decision making, one that is contrary to his personal inclinations:

> **George:** I'll tell you this: something is happening in my life! I did this opposite thing last night. Up was down! Black was white! Good was . . .
> **Jerry:** . . . bad.
> **George:** Day was . . .
> **Elaine:** . . . night.

The sad thing for George is that he only followed "The Opposite" for one episode and promptly returned to ruminating about his life rather than changing his behavior. By the end of the episode, he is back to his old self, complete with conflict and dissatisfaction:

Elaine: How're things going? You wanna know how things are going? I'll tell you how things are going. I am getting kicked out of my apartment!

Jerry: Why? Why are they doing that?

Elaine: I don't know! They have a list of grievances.

Jerry: The jewel thief?

Elaine: Yeah, the jewel thief.

Jerry: What else?

Elaine: I put Canadian quarters in the washing machine. I gotta be out by the end of the month.

George: Well, you could move in with my parents.

Elaine: Was that the . . . opposite . . . of what you were going to say, or was that just instinct? [She squeezes George's mouth between her fingers.]

George: Instinct.

Elaine: Stick . . . with the opposite. [Slaps George on the forehead.]

When I am dealing with my ADHD clients, I take great pains to follow Elaine's advice. I definitely stick with the opposite. Even though I am an ADHDer myself, I have the same impulses as everybody else to scold, criticize, and even lose my temper at the behaviors and decisions of my clients. I have learned—with help from meditation, mindfulness techniques, and therapy—to observe my impulses and then make a different, more productive response.

STOP THE INSANITY!

When you realize that your efforts have not yielded results, you must stop what you've been doing. You must end the insanity of repeating ineffective behaviors. As a parent or loved one, you've been so plugged in to the shortcomings of the ADHDer in your life that you have probably lost objectivity. You have worried so much about school or career performance that you have failed to realize that your relationship has suffered.

Out of deep concern for your child, you have doggedly tracked missing assignments, upcoming projects, and tests. You have checked the planner every day to make sure it was filled in and have regularly communicated with teachers to make sure nothing slipped under the radar. If he or she won't take responsibility, you reason, somebody has to do it. You just want your child to live up to his or her potential. Who can fault you for that?

But now is the time to let go. This is the first "opposite" that you need to put in place. This process inserts some space between you and your loved one. Think of it as a "no-man's-land." You have to lay off for a little while before implementing new strategies. You are interrupting long-standing patterns, which powerfully communicates to your loved one that things are going to shift. You are modeling change instead of trying to force it.

My clients have an especially hard time following this seemingly simple piece of advice. Old habits die hard. They intend to follow my recommendations, but often they cannot resist the urge to insert themselves into their loved one's "problems." Kathy, a successful attorney, brought her ADHD son to see me because of his low grades and obsession with the online computer game *World of Warcraft*. When we met the first time, she took out a stack of color-coded file folders with his report cards, progress reports, and psychological testing going back to second grade. To deal with the ADHD tendency toward disorganization, parents like Kathy become hyper-organized to compensate. She had so much invested in her son's success that it was incredibly difficult for her to let go.

Kathy's son pointed out at our second meeting that his mother had not honored her commitment to stay out of his school affairs. "She's not doing what she promised," he said. "She leaves me at least ten notes a day and has even learned how to send text messages, which she said she could never figure out before." Kathy had employed new-and-improved methods, but was still intruding. It was almost as though the behaviors had become hardwired within her.

THE TRUTH SETS YOU FREE

Even though Kathy struggled to stay out of her son's schoolwork, she was so committed to helping him succeed that she was always open to my advice. It is not a stretch to say that Kathy had been compulsive about her son's progress in school. "When I'm at work," she told me, "I can't resist the urge to go on the school website and check his grades and see if he has any missing assignments." Before they came to see me, she used to print out his grade reports every day and highlight missing assignments. Those highlighted in yellow were high priority and those in pink meant that they were too late to get credit, although Kathy insisted they still be completed. Blue highlighting was for the assignments her son had lost points on simply because of the work not being done completely or on time. She would sometimes draw frowning faces next to these. She was oblivious to how angry this highlighting ritual had made her son.

"I hate those papers," he told me. "My friend has a fire pit in his backyard and I use it to burn everything my mom prints out." He had all but stopped talking to his mother and was a very angry young man. I was able, over a short time, to convince him to tell his mother how he really felt. She was shocked. She could not believe that actions she saw as loving and helpful had actually alienated him. To her credit, she realized that, before she tried to help her son, she needed to examine her own issues. She said, "I don't know why I didn't see any of this before."

Like Kathy, most people who bring their loved ones to me are highly motivated and willing to go to extraordinary lengths to help. But they rarely recognize that to help their ADHDer, they must first help themselves. "Being organized was the best thing I ever did in school," Kathy said. "I just wanted to give my son all the tools and advantages I had." She failed to see that her way of being organized was never going to work for her son. She tried to get him to tackle problems the way she did, and he rebelled. If you do not want a full-scale rebellion on your hands, then do not try to pigeonhole your child into certain methods simply because they worked for you. Your ADHD loved one is not you!

It amazes me how many parents with an ADHD child have the condition themselves. Of course, research shows that ADHD runs in families. In spite of this, ADHD parents with an ADHD child are often quite intolerant. In most cases, the parent had discovered workable strategies for his or her own life, and they're usually not the ones that will work for the child.

Many of the adults I help are very successful businesspeople. ADHD individuals often make great entrepreneurs. They thrive on innovation and are not afraid to take risks. Although these tendencies can be put to good use in business ventures, they likewise create problems at home.

Typically, I start seeing the child with ADHD first. Through the course of my work, I often uncover problems in the home. Fourteen-year-old Kyle came to me because of his failing grades. In addition to ADHD, the young man suffered from severe anxiety. The first hints of trouble came when he was attending one of my ADHD Study Groups. He called his father because he had forgotten his Spanish workbook. Kyle's face quickly turned into a snarl. His tone was demanding and he expressed indignation that his father was not going to rush right over with the book. After perhaps thirty seconds of this, his father exploded, and I could hear it from twenty-five feet away through a cell phone earpiece!

> *ADHD that presents with anxiety is often tricky to treat because of its many unique difficulties. The stimulant medications, for example, do not work well on ADHDers who also have anxiety (like me). Research is starting to suggest that this represents a distinct subtype of the disorder.*[9]

George, Kyle's father, owned four businesses: two trucking companies, a medical supply company, and a medical billing operation. "I have the ideas," he told me. "I work incredibly hard to get the business off the ground. Then I turn it over to someone who can manage it." George worked with his ADHD. He knew his weaknesses and surrounded himself with staff who could compensate. If anything got in his way, George went at it like a steamroller. This approach has great benefits in business, but does not work well at home. "When he doesn't like something that we do," his wife Sharon said, "George's first impulse is to yell. It's almost like he enjoys chaos, and Kyle is getting to be the same way." Kyle had been in trouble many times for yelling at teachers. Unlike his father, he had not developed compensatory strategies for his ADHD. His anxiety seemed to fuel his anger, and the whole family stayed angry most of the time. Before I could do anything to help them, I sent them to a family therapist. Sometimes families are so broken that there is little I can do to help until they're made whole again.

Kyle's family was at the point that they were willing to be helped, but things had just gotten too out of control. They were in an enveloping morass of negativity. Their example argues for earlier rather than later intervention.

ADHD carries a great risk for creating family chaos. As I sit back and consider my recommendations, I realize that it is incredibly easy to make these pronouncements and even easier to read them. Most people find that putting them into practice requires a daily commitment to change. Over the years, I have tried out a host of methods on myself and recommended what worked to parents and loved ones of my clients. Most people, including myself, stumble a lot on the road to personal transformation.

COMING OUT OF DENIAL

By the time families come to me, they're usually in crisis. I tell them what one of my mentors, John Everingham, told me very early in my own journey of personal growth: "For the Chinese, the ideograph for 'crisis' is made up of two characters: one that signifies 'danger,' and the other, 'opportunity.'" Although this maxim is actually a somewhat bad translation, I have found wisdom in it. So, if you are in crisis right now, it is important to keep in mind that you also have a precious opportunity for change, perhaps even transformation.

The most significant periods of growth in my life were preceded by great uncertainty. In my teens and early twenties, for instance, I was a chain-smoking ball of anxiety and possessed enormous creative energy that had no place to go. I prided myself, though, on my academic and intellectual achievements. As my college days came to a close, I was forced to dismount my high horse of intellectual superiority and finally admit that I had a lot of problems to work on. I had used the prepackaged structure that university life provided to avoid dealing with my many issues. Stripped of that security blanket, I was confronted with feelings of shame, insecurity, and the hard-to-admit realization that I had no idea what I wanted to do with my life.

Not only did I have no career path in mind, but I also had no idea how to begin the process of feeling better about myself. My strategy had been to work hard in school. I temporarily felt good about myself because "I was smart" and "I was at the top of my class." The reassurance such self-talk had provided was gone.

Life in high school and college had hummed along, but just two months after I graduated from college in December 1993, I suddenly felt lost and every day became a struggle. The reservoir of unresolved issues spilled over and demanded attention. At the time, it seemed like the very fabric of my life was unraveling, but now I can see that I was simply experiencing the pain that invariably ensues when people come out of denial. In February 1994, I slept sixteen hours a day and had to force myself to eat. I was lucky that my friend Dave let me stay with him. A professor of Spanish and linguistics, he was someone I really trusted. He shared my love of learning foreign languages and, like me, had grown up without a father. I felt deeply connected to him, and I would even say that he was, in many ways, the father I never had. He convinced me that what I was experiencing had been a part of me all along and that I was finally allowing myself to feel it. Being around Dave was like having my own attentive, always-available therapist. His devotion brought me back from the brink of clinical depression. He inspired me to work on myself and, incidentally, insisted that I would someday be a writer!

I pursued personal growth with the same all-encompassing vigor I had directed toward school. I started spending a large portion of my scant earnings on weekend workshops, seminars, and spiritual trainings. I quickly became what a friend of mine dubbed a "self-help junkie."

Looking back on those early years of personal growth, I see that being stripped of my sense of security was ultimately a gift. It slapped me in the face and told me that it was time to look within. If you are in a position in which your efforts to help your loved one have failed, maybe you have been given a gift. Perhaps, contrary to your initial assumptions, this is an opportunity for you to grow. Your impulse has been to focus all of your efforts on your loved one. It is now time to stop that and do the opposite: work on yourself!

When your loved one sees you questioning your motives and behaviors, you will, once again, be the model for change instead of the enforcer.

SHIFTING THE BALANCE OF POWER

When you start to see your situation as a possible gift, the next step is to slow down and observe your reactions without acting on them. This sounds much simpler than it actually is. For most of us, anger does not feel like an option. Yelling at our kids feels less like a choice and more like a duty. Like the father I mentioned earlier, you can start the process by keeping a response journal. You simply keep track of how you respond to your loved one and use a handheld tape recorder to get a more accurate rendering of the intensity of your reactions. The simple fact of knowing you are recording yourself will also make you more aware!

When you think you have an accurate assessment of your behavior, you might want to show your list to your loved one and ask his or her opinion:

- Does this list seem accurate to you?

- Did I include everything?

- Is there anything I left out?

- What would you add?

When you explain what you are doing, you will get his or her attention. I have seen this simple technique totally transform lives. It can reverse the power dynamic. Many people, on the other hand, nag their ADHD loved one for failure to live up to imposed standards without holding themselves to those same standards. ADHD folks are extremely sensitive to power dynamics, which is one reason we are so good at resisting.

If you have implemented my advice thus far, you have taken a great leap in sidestepping your ADHDer's resistance. Rather than fighting for control, you have entered a new dimension. To stay there, you must be vigilant.

THE MONASTERY OF THE MIND

"Inside myself is a place where I live all alone and that is where I renew my springs that never dry up."
—Pearl S. Buck, Nobel laureate

Throughout my life, people have described me as hyperactive, loud, goofy, and too intense—and those are the people who like me! Those close to me were shocked in 2001 when I signed up for a ten-day, mostly silent monastic retreat. My therapist had convinced me that I "needed to slow down." When she suggested that a long meditation retreat might help me, I signed up. Looking back, I was already putting the "opposite" into action, because the essence of the retreat was basically "sit down, shut up, and stare at your belly button." For me, a loud-mouthed ball of anxiety with rapidly shifting attention, this was the opposite of every impulse I had ever had. I had no idea what was in store for me and was actually excited as I, along with my two traveling companions, drove the four hours to the secluded commune where the retreat was to take place. I wanted to feel better about myself and get some direction in my life, and my therapist had done a masterful job of convincing me that this was the ticket. I went into the experience with expectant faith.

As I waited with the other participants for the event to start, I realized that I, at age twenty-five, was the youngest attendee by fifteen years. I was surrounded by veterans of virtually every new age workshop that one could imagine. There were Harikrishna rejects, crystal worshippers, Native American wannabes, and so-called Buddhists (Buddhism was in great fashion at that time). "I don't belong here," I told myself. "These people are real freaks, even by my self-help-junkie standards." The "helpers" on staff all spoke in a deliberate and earnest manner reminiscent of grade-school teachers. I found them nauseating.

As I struggled to invent a legitimate reason to leave, the retreat master, an American who called himself Manoj, rang a bell and called us together. "You are all here," he began his remarks, "because you are getting tired of the incessant ramblings of the 'monkey mind.'" I had no idea what he was talking about, and I was wishing I had driven alone so I could get the heck out of there. I was sure that their insistence that participants carpool was a ruse to make it difficult for people to leave.

I had no choice but to stay. I suffered through interminable meditation sittings, endured hour-long chanting sessions of the syllable "ram," and had to listen to people "share" over and over again from their journals. It was the closest I had come to duplicating the hellish boredom of grade school.

On the fifth day of the monotony, however, something shifted. We spent the whole day alone in our rooms with a candle, a journal, and a pen. It was called "The Day of Solitude." I still do not understand what happened, but about halfway through the day, after I had feverishly written in my journal in an effort to channel my nervous energy, suddenly a distance opened up between me and my thoughts. I actually started "watching" my thoughts instead of being possessed by them. My attention kept shifting, as it always does, but I began to observe these shifts, as if a part of me were at a distance, just gazing upon the frequent movements of my mind.

Until then, I had already tried numerous therapies, seminars, workshops, retreats, and spiritual disciplines. None of them had succeeded in getting me to slow down. But this experience, as aggravating as it was, gave me a harbor of calm. This inner sense has stayed with me ever since. A "storm" can be raging around me, and I can always find a place of peace within. This serves me in my work with ADHD kids, and it has helped me focus my energies in a way that medication, retreats, and therapy could not.

Medication

When people talk to me about ADHD, the conversation almost always turns to medication. First of all, young people's experience with medication tends to be more positive than negative.[10] However, many of my students and clients experience effects that can make it difficult to stay on their meds: loss of appetite (and weight), sleep disruptions, personality changes, agitated feelings, and increased anxiety, to name a few. I personally know of cases in which ADHDers have sold their medication for profit. I have, however, seen ADHD medications greatly transform lives. If you choose to go the route of medication, the best advice I can give is to find a very good, experienced psychiatrist or pediatrician who comes highly recommended. Once your loved one begins taking the medication, be on the lookout for positive and negative developments. Also, be aware that your ADHD loved one may make it look like he or she is taking the medication, when in fact the pills end up in the trash. ADHD medications are strong drugs that affect the functioning of the brain. Great caution and awareness are therefore advised.

My message to you is that you need to find that harbor of tranquility within yourself. You might find it through religion, yoga, meditation, or even simple daily rituals like beginning your day with a walk through a park. I cannot tell you how to get to that inner peaceful place, but I can tell you that you will benefit from it once you find it.

I begin every day with a short meditation and a gratitude list. Meditation helps me cultivate calm, and the gratitude list helps me start the day with a positive mindset. I simply start a new page in my notebook and write down all the things I am grateful for. I seem to naturally focus on the negative, so being grateful helps me balance things out.

I don't recommend any one particular practice, but I do suggest that you spend some time researching and trying different approaches. If Kevin Roberts can find peace, then so can you, but it is something that you have to cultivate and work on every day. Don't just do what I have done. You have to find your own way, so get out there and start experimenting! You have to find practices, disciplines, and rituals that work for you.

SEEKING SUPPORT

As important as solitude is to help ground oneself and observe one's reactions, it is equally important to create and maintain a network of support. Such a network can take many forms. Several layers of support seem to be most effective. Kathy, the hyper-organized mother, for example, discovered that another attorney in her firm was also dealing with an ADHD child. The two of them had lunch once a week and discussed their successes and failures and also called each other for advice during particularly stressful times. In addition, Kathy joined a monthly parent support group run by a local chapter of CHADD (Children and Adults with Attention Deficit/Hyperactivity Disorder). As part of her involvement with CHADD, she also participated in a series of classes called "Parent to Parent." She felt this program was most valuable. "Only parents who have dealt with ADHD understand what you're going through," she told me. "Parent to Parent gave me tangible skills that I was able to practice after one week's training and then get feedback on my progress the next week. It was incredible!"

Kathy also felt it beneficial to see a therapist. "My reactions to my son," she said, "showed me that I had issues of my own that I was putting on him. I had to do my own work before I could help him." It was in therapy that Kathy discovered her own ADHD. Some parents of ADHDers find, as Kathy did, that they, too, suffer from ADHD. It is only after their children are diagnosed, in many cases, that they uncover the key to many of the difficulties they had experienced throughout their lives. They often find that the frustration they experience toward their children is exacerbated by the mounds of frustration they feel toward themselves. Through therapy and support groups like CHADD, these parents are able to disentangle their own issues from those of their children. Their responses to negative behaviors become more appropriate to the needs of the situation and fueled less by their unresolved emotional issues.

People who succeed in positively changing the relationship with their ADHDer employ several levels of support. The more support you get, the more successful you will be.

To sum it all up, the important ingredients for changing your relationship with the ADHDer in your life are these:

- identifying your ineffective reactions
- stopping ineffective reactions
- self-reflection
- support
- new responses and strategies

Once you have identified and stopped your ineffective responses, you must deal with your own issues and establish a strong support network. With that base of strength firmly established, you can then think about increasing your arsenal of new skills and strategies.

CHAPTER 4

THE OPPOSITE IN ACTION

*"Take the course opposite to custom
and you will almost always do well."*
Jean-Jacques Rousseau, French writer, philosopher

I have amassed an armory of ADHD-approved methods, drawing on my own experiences as a student in school, four years as a classroom teacher, and the last thirteen years as an ADHD and academic coach. I now run what I call ADHD Study Groups. Kids come for a period of three to four hours—sometimes longer—and we do schoolwork, take video game breaks, eat pizza, and have fun, which is the most important aspect. Participants learn the important lesson that succeeding in school does not necessarily involve drudgery, frustration, and boredom.

Study Groups have provided me with an amazing laboratory for experimentation. The wide variety of ADHD types I regularly encounter necessitates an ongoing development of strategies. I still regularly run across new students who stump me, a situation that sends me back to the drawing board to develop fresh tactics. Innovation is a necessity in my work.

My strong suit in these groups is creativity, but I also have a secret weapon: I am not a family member. As you contemplate new methods and strategies, it is important to keep in mind that the ADHDer in your life may not take your suggestions. In fact, the strategies I recommend had often been suggested by parents or loved ones; the ADHD folks were just not willing to try them until they started working with me.

To have any hope of getting an ADHDer to try new methods, you will have to employ "The Opposite." As you saw in the last chapter, you must tread quite carefully. Before you put a plan in place, ask yourself these questions:

- Is your ADHDer going to be open to suggestions from you?

- Have you done enough of your own personal growth work to make sure that you are not repeating the same worn-out patterns?

- Have you already tried to help the individual implement new strategies but failed?

- Is there somebody else in the family, or a family friend, from whom advice would be better received?

- Do you need to hire a professional to help you with implementation?

- Could it be useful to find a local high school or college student to serve as a tutor or mentor? Is there a support group from which your loved one would benefit?

I have seen parents and loved ones work on themselves and the relationship with their ADHDer to such an admirable extent that they were able to help implement new strategies. But more typically, I have seen folks sincerely try to help with new strategies only to create more conflict. If you're dealing with a preteen, it will be much easier to repair the interpersonal bridge and forge ahead with new strategies. With a teenager, young adult, or adult, however, the transition will likely be rocky. He or she has been resisting help for many years, and the barriers that have been erected will prove tricky to break down.

"A PROPHET IS NOT RECOGNIZED IN HIS OWN LAND" (GOSPEL OF MATTHEW 13:57)

You may be like the prophets in ancient times who had great ideas about how people should run their lives differently but encountered resistance and scorn from those who knew them best. Jesus started a religion that now counts more than two billion followers, yet at the time friends and neighbors from his village wanted to run him out of town (Luke 4:28–30). Familiarity often breeds contempt. Aware of this fact, you may need to face the hard-to-accept reality that you are never going to be the "savior" for the ADHDer in your life. In such circumstances, you could employ the services of a coach, tutor, or therapist. These options can be expensive, however.

If you're trying to help a child, one inexpensive option is to find a parent with whom you can "exchange children." At first glance, this may sound odd. I have had several parents of modest means help their kids turn things around with just this approach. Working with someone else's child is usually a lot easier than working with your own. Think of how many times other parents have told you how helpful and polite your child was. Yet, at home, you have to practically scream at him or her to have any hope that a chore will get done. Many parents have exploited this behavioral discrepancy to great effect.

Kathy and Becca, two single mothers, had sons who had been friends since kindergarten. Both boys turned out to be ADHD. By sixth grade, the two mothers came under great strain, because their sons did not respond well to the added pressures and responsibilities of middle school. Supporting their sons in grade school had been far simpler. The mothers had received daily streams of homework and progress information from their sons' homeroom teachers, and behavioral issues were relatively minor. Those problems that did arise were dealt with compassionately by a principal who had taken the time to get to know the boys and who was emotionally invested in their success. With five different teachers to deal with in middle school, the mothers' academic support roles drastically increased in complexity, and Becca's son began to receive detentions. Neither mother had the monetary means to hire outside help. To make matters worse, both had meager health insurance policies that did not cover very many visits to a therapist. I met Becca at a conference at which I was giving a seminar on "The Opposite." I realized Becca had been attentively listening to my speech when at the end, after telling me her story, she asked, "What is 'the opposite' that I should follow?" I did not have a ready answer but told her I would think about it.

A SOLUTION CLOSE TO HOME

Becca and I e-mailed back and forth for several weeks. She lived more than an hour away from me, so e-mail and phone were the only practical options for staying in touch. Becca and I scoured her area for social services and did not find many viable options for her son and his friend. I tried to find therapists and psychiatrists in her area to take on the boys pro bono but was not successful. Becca found a man from her church who was willing to be a mentor to her son, but his lack of empathy and understanding of ADHD created more conflict than his help was worth. The local library had some free tutoring, but neither boy was well suited to the hushed tones required of them in such an environment. After more than two months of exhaustive searching, I had an idea that prompted me to call Becca immediately. "Perhaps the solution has been under our noses the whole time," I told her. "You and Kathy already help and support each other. All you have to do is take it one step further."

I suggested a child exchange. The two women were skeptical but were willing to give it a try. Becca picked up Josh, Kathy's son, after school, and Kathy picked up Derek, Becca's son. Josh and Derek were not allowed to return to their own houses until both of them had completed all homework. This element of the plan created a healthy rivalry between the boys, because if one lagged in homework completion, the other was stuck without access to the electronic creature comforts of home that many kids now rely on. In addition, they both started to use the learning resource center at school more effectively, because they knew that they were not going to be able to go home until all work was finished. It gave them incentive to get as much work done at school as possible. Lack of effective use of school time now had a natural, and highly irritating, consequence.

The arrangement added much-needed academic motivation. Temper tantrums and arguing about homework all but ceased. Kathy said, "It's easier to enforce rules with Derek than it is with my own son. He doesn't fight me on everything like Josh does." Each boy also proved more willing to ask for and accept help with homework and studying. "I don't have to bicker with Josh on every little detail," Becca said. "Things just run a lot more smoothly." After a few weeks of this approach, the two mothers began alternating responsibility for communicating with teachers so that they each received a break from that duty every other week. Luckily, the boys had the same teachers for all classes but one. This practice helped to lighten the load on both mothers. Kathy said, "Both boys still have difficulties, but exchanging kids has helped the two of us keep our sanity. The boys are definitely more successful in school too."

If you want to take the approach used by Kathy and Becca, joining CHADD (Children and Adults with Attention Deficit/Hyperactivity Disorder) will give you access to a large group of parents who experience problems similar to yours. You can find a local chapter through CHADD's website: www.chadd.org. The national office phone number is 301-306-7070. CHADD offers conferences, support groups, and the sympathetic ear of parents who share similar struggles. The group's national conference draws experts from around the world. I highly recommend attending. Local chapters of CHADD give you access to incredibly wise and compassionate people.

LOCAL RESOURCES

After three months had passed, Kathy worked out an arrangement with the moderator of the local high school's National Merit Society, a group whose members excel academically but who are also required to volunteer in the community. One day per week, Josh and Derek worked on homework for a few hours with two high school junior boys who were assigned to them. After homework was finished, the older boys often hung around and played video games and, on a few occasions, took the younger boys to play laser tag. Josh and Derek benefited immensely from the mentoring of the older boys, because they were seen as "cool," and schoolwork was thus seen as a lot more fun. Given the scant contact that both boys had with their fathers, the high schoolers also filled in as much-needed male role models. Positive role models are especially important for ADHDers, because self-esteem issues often push them toward the "bad kids" and underachievers. I strongly encourage parents to find mentors and role models at church, local high schools, and even Big Brothers Big Sisters. One particularly powerful organization is the Boys and Girls Clubs of America, which has clubs centered mostly around urban areas throughout the country.

I was a member of a Boys and Girls Club and received some incredibly powerful mentoring, guidance, and leadership training. Tim Kowalski, the director at my club, took a special interest in me. When I was eleven, I started spending time with the "bad kids" and showed signs of antisocial and destructive behavior. Tim took me aside on a regular basis and tried to knock some sense into me. One thing he said still lives with me. "Kevin," he said, "you are definitely going to be a leader in life. You have to decide whether you want to be a good leader who helps people or a bad leader who causes them pain." As I wrote that just now, I got shivers up my back and down my arms. I can still feel the power of his statement resound within me. Without Tim Kowalski and the Boys and Girls Club, there's no telling the trouble I would have gotten into. I say without hesitation that the Boys and Girls Club saved my life. The organization offers athletics, homework clubs, leadership training, and an incredibly diverse set of activities and programs, not to mention a talented and devoted staff. Its website is www.bgca.org.

Becca and Kathy did not have a Boys and Girls Club near them, but they still managed to find some good role models. Like many ADHD kids, their sons would have been considered "at risk." The actions of these two mothers probably prevented a great deal of destructive and deviant behavior.

Kathy and Becca's story demonstrates the power of creativity and perseverance. Both qualities are crucial in confronting the complexity that invariably arises with ADHD. Kathy and Becca accepted that they were not the right people to help their respective sons. Without spending much money, they came up with workable solutions. They did not rest on their laurels when the "child exchange" brought improvement to their sons' academic performances. They continuously sought new ways to augment that approach. Creativity with ADHD must be an ongoing process, because once a system gets stale and predictable, ADHDers struggle to stay with it.

KEEPING IT FRESH

I advocate employing a variety of strategies and mixing them up from time to time. I follow my own advice in this matter. When I am at home and experience writer's block, I sometimes simply switch computers. I might even write for a while standing up. If these tricks do not work, I take my laptop and go to the food court at a local mall. Sometimes I thrive with a certain degree of ambient noise, but other times it drives me crazy. On occasion, I go the gym and work out on an elliptical machine or treadmill. I often get great ideas when I exercise, so I keep a handheld digital recorder at the ready so I don't forget anything. I always have a recorder in the car, because I seem to be at my intellectual best when I am driving. Many sections of this book were written from ramblings I recorded while rushing down the freeway!

I am consistent in that I, with purpose and intention, constantly vary my routine and strategies to stay focused. I employ this same wisdom with my students. If one method works with an ADHDer, I never assume that it will continue to work.

As you learn about the tools in this book, you may find one strategy that functions particularly well. If you do not mix it up with other approaches, however, it will probably stop working. "He was doing so well when he studied on the treadmill," Danny's mother said, "but now he doesn't want to do it anymore. I can't understand that." The only thing that she needed to understand is that, although ADHDers require structure, they usually resist routine. It goes back to that need for novel stimulation to keep the brain active. Routine and structure must be balanced with novelty and excitement.

Although I am a strong advocate of varying routine, it is also important to find a few core behaviors that remain constant. I keep track of appointments and meetings with my cell phone calendar, which then reminds me by ringing at a specified time. If I make a commitment, I immediately take out my cell phone, enter the date and time, and program two reminders—one for the night before and one for two hours before. This system works, and I follow it faithfully. Since I started using my cell phone calendar, I have missed very few appointments. I also write for thirty minutes every single day, and a cell phone reminder goes off three times a day to make sure I have put in my time. I exercise a minimum of three days a week because aerobic activity is the most powerful ADHD "drug" that I have ever experienced. These constants give me a core of structure that keeps me engaged. Like most ADHDers, I can easily slip into a pit of TV and Internet sloth. When I indulge in these unproductive behaviors, I end up feeling very bad about myself, which then sends me into a downward spiral. Whereas adults used to point out how I fell short in school and life, I now beat up on myself. Following a core of positive behaviors on a daily basis helps me to not do that.

CREATIVELY FINDING THE OPPOSITE

As I have said many times during the last thirteen years, being ADHD often feels like having an ever-present, giant finger pointing at you. We ADHD folks get so accustomed to scolding and scorn that we develop unconscious mechanisms designed to divert oncoming criticism. Remember that our deception, lying, and "creative storytelling" are all rooted in conflict avoidance, so please stop taking our behaviors personally. This recommendation is surely easier said than done, but "The Opposite" will serve you well.

Marcia was one of those mothers who thought about her ADHD son day and night but could not "get" him to change. When she heard about "The Opposite" from a friend of hers who had attended one of my lectures, she called me and we started off together on a five-month odyssey. My work with Marcia greatly increased my "opposite" repertoire.

During our first conversation, she said, "The hair on the back of my neck stood up when my friend told me about this 'opposite' thing. I knew that nothing I had done to help my son with his ADHD had ever really worked, so I thought maybe I needed to do the opposite." Marcia hired me to be her personal coach, and we talked by phone every day for three months. Our discussions took place at ten thirty at night. She used our half hour to dissect her responses and reactions to her son's behavior that had occurred during the previous day or two. We would then brainstorm ways that she could respond more effectively in the future. One topic came up repeatedly. Marcia, like many a parent with an ADHD child, struggled a great deal with nagging. She felt an irresistible impulse to track her son's commitments and then constantly remind him. "I did it again," she would begin our coaching call, deeply frustrated at her inability to let go. "What's the opposite of nagging?" she asked. I told her that there were many possible opposites, but asked her to try out one that seemed particularly appropriate to her situation: silence.

THE SILENT TREATMENT

ADHDers are masters at getting people to react. You resist our efforts, and we uncover even sneakier ways of sailing under your radar. We have instinctual powers to find that one button that needs pushing. Snap! We get you to yell at us yet again. I receive frustrating e-mails every day from parents who cannot stop yelling at their kids. It took Marcia months to learn not to react. But she kept at it, and the relationship with her son improved significantly, which contributed to Marcia's ability to convince her son to willingly see a therapist and work with an ADHD coach a few days a week. "When I learned to keep my mouth shut," Marcia said, "my son actually started to listen to me."

One father, Mike, experienced troubles similar to Marcia's. He told me, "When I find out Eric lied to me, I have to yell at him, or I feel like I'm being a bad parent." I met with Mike and Eric and witnessed the broken state of their relationship. They engaged in a seemingly scripted volley of back-and-forth criticism, defensive retorts, and outrage. With the two of them in the same room, it was impossible to make any progress. I decided to start working with the father alone.

Mike was a certified public accountant. He was paid to find mistakes and efficiently fix them. Mike saw the glass as half empty, a mindset that I'm sure helped in his career. He took his work home with him, focusing on the problems and inadequacies of his son, and usually ignored progress and small victories. "I don't mind that my son has problems," he said. "But what gets me is that he doesn't seem to do anything to solve them. I worked hard to have a better life than my father, but my son is lazy. His sense of entitlement drives me crazy." Adding to his frustration, Mike felt deep down that he was a failure as a parent. He put a lot of energy into his son without much in the way of results. I asked him, "Do you think you're helping Eric by reacting to him like you do?" He responded, "I just want him to do well." Of course, he had not answered the question. I pushed him, and he finally admitted, "You're right. I've been yelling at him and criticizing for years, and things have gotten worse. What else can

I do?" Mike realized he had no other tools to rely on. Growing up, he had reacted to his own father very differently. When his father yelled at him, Mike responded, more or less, by changing his behavior. The application of a negative stimulus (yelling) resulted in Mike altering his behavior over time to avoid his father's wrath. When Mike yelled at Eric, the young man's behavior only became more entrenched. The boy clearly did not play by the same rules his father had unconsciously internalized. Using business jargon that I thought Mike would understand, I told him, "You need to start thinking outside of the box."

Mike was a big boxing fan, so I continued my point with one of my favorite Muhammad Ali quotes: "Silence is golden when you can't think of a good answer." I printed out the quote in a twenty-eight-point font and made several copies, instructing him to put them on his bathroom mirror, in his car, and on his desk at work. Keeping quiet was such a tall order for Mike that he needed constant reminders. In addition, he had a standing appointment to call me on the way home from work so that I could prepare him to not react to the disappointing news that likely awaited him when he walked in the door. "Your job, Mike," I told him forthrightly, "is to shut up."

Before anything else, father and son needed to repair their relationship. Constant criticism exacts a heavy toll. Silence is like a "no fly zone" or a "no-man's-land." It halts "hostilities" and thus gives the relationship space so healing can slowly begin. After about a week of relative silence, Mike's son asked, "Dad, why are you not saying anything about school?" Mike responded, "Because what I was saying made things worse. I care more about our relationship than I do about your schoolwork."

IT GETS WORSE BEFORE IT GETS BETTER

Mike's son initially responded to his father's silence by intensifying his efforts to get a reaction. This is to be expected. As Daniel Amen has pointed out, ADHDers come to unconsciously rely on negativity in relationships to increase activity in their brains.[1] By curtailing his yelling and criticism, Mike had "deprived" his son of a reliable source of brain stimulation. The young man had become dependent on the negativity and desperately—although unconsciously—tried to get it back. He swore at his father, threw temper tantrums, and insulted one of his teachers, prompting three days of in-school suspension and a series of meetings his father had to attend.

Faced with this barrage of acting out, Mike suffered a few setbacks. He did blow up at his son a few times. He was a goal-oriented man and was terribly hard on himself. "I feel like a volcano," Mike said, "and every time I do not respond, the lava gets closer to the surface. Eric knows how to get to me more than anyone I have ever met." Eric knew, mostly unconsciously, that if he pushed hard enough, he could still get a rise out of his father, thus keeping the cycle of negativity alive.

Mike succeeded in holding back his anger 90 percent of the time, but a 10-percent failure rate was enough to prevent progress. To have any hope of success, Mike needed to find a way to release the rage that regularly built up within him, or the whole plan would fail.

DISCHARGE NEGATIVITY

I suggested a few techniques to help Mike discharge his emotions before they got out of control. He decided to set up a punching bag in his basement and made a ritual out of using it every night after work. "You have to honor your anger, Mike," I told him. "If you try to ignore anger, it will control you and could destroy your family." Punching the bag with his rage allowed Mike to take more responsibility for his anger. As this process evolved, Mike learned that his anger was not just about his son. "I put on a happy face at the office every day," Mike said. "But you know what? A lot of those people really piss me off." He had never gotten angry at work. He "saved" it for his son. "You know, I think that some of the rage I expressed at my son really had nothing to do with him," Mike confessed. "But when I would find out about his goof-ups in school, it was like the straw that broke the camel's back." Realizing the true scope of his anger made Mike a much more conscious and self-reflective individual, qualities that helped immensely in dealing with his son. He also took my advice and started seeing a therapist for anger management.

Mike justified ranting at his son by positively recollecting his own father's parenting style. As he became more aware, however, Mike saw things about his father that he had previously denied. "My father did the same thing," he told me. "Everybody at the office thought he was the greatest guy in the world, but he would come home and start yelling at us almost immediately." Unlike his own father, Mike stopped displacing his anger on his son. He discharged it into an inanimate object and discovered a great many things about himself. He learned that, although his son did things that were wrong, Mike's expression of anger was a choice. He learned to accept responsibility for his own choices.

Marcia, from the earlier story, approached her frustration with her son in a slightly different manner. At first, she tried yoga. She wanted to attain inner peace so that she wouldn't feel any anger at all. Although doing yoga calmed her, she reluctantly admitted that her anger was not going away. She switched to tae kwon do. "I've come to the conclusion that I will probably always have some anger," she said. "Tae kwon do gives me a way to channel it so that anger is not a major part of my relationship with my son."

Sandy, a mother of an oppositional-defiant fourteen-year-old ADHD boy, channeled her anger by beating pillows with a tennis racket in her garage. She went out there every day before her son came home and sometimes required supplementary "racket work" after interacting with him. She said, "I can feel my anger well up inside long before I get to the point of yelling at my son. Working with the racket has allowed me to be with my anger without letting it control me. I no longer blame my son for my getting out of control." She modeled a relatively healthy way of dealing with bottled-up rage.

Each parent must find a practice that works for him or her. I advise experimenting with a few different approaches to see which one works best. Several strategies can be used in tandem, of course. If you do try to use the tennis-racket approach or something similar, wear gloves, make sure no one else is around, and be careful! Sandy admits to having had a few "accidents"! You can definitely hurt yourself. If you get to the point that you feel the need to hit a person, however, it might be time to find a good therapist, and it couldn't hurt to get one well versed in anger management.

Some people, like Mike, have had such major issues that I have had to refer them to anger management. If a parent has a pre-existing anger problem, an ADHD child will have an easy time pushing him or her over the edge. In addition, anger-prone children often arise from anger-prone parents. Ten sessions with an anger management therapist are often sufficient to get things under control. Angry parental outbursts damage a child's self-esteem and increase the risk that the child will have anger issues as an adult. When this dynamic operates between spouses, it can easily destroy a relationship.

> *Studies continue to show that the way that we perceive the stressors in our lives affects our experience and expression of strong negative emotions, such as anger.[2] This is the reason education about ADHD is so important. The way you perceive ADHD has a clear impact on the emotions you end up experiencing from the stressful interactions you have with the ADHDer in your life.*

RESPOND, BUT DO NOT REACT

"The longer I live, the more convinced I become that life is ten percent what happens to us and ninety percent how we respond."
—Charles Swindoll, American writer and clergyman

After a "honeymoon" period when kids first start working with me, many of them end up treating me like one of their parents. I have encounters every day in which I discover kids lied to me or that they did not follow through on a commitment, and sometimes they hurl insults at me. My success in dealing with such behavior depends largely on my responses. Usually, I practice what I preach by waiting a few seconds before I respond. I let my anger percolate, but I have learned to simply let it be there without acting on it.

Some children present particularly potent challenges, however. Michael, a fourteen-year-old, has not only ADHD but Asperger's syndrome as well. Like many with this condition, he is highly oppositional and defiant. His IQ is off the charts, and he uses his superior intellect to manipulate. He challenges every microscopic detail and assumes that he is in charge of any and every situation.

"I need help on my math *right now*," he demanded, as if I were his slave. He had interrupted me while I was intensely focused on editing a girl's English paper, a process during which all the kids know I hate to be interrupted. I really get angry when my focus is rudely disturbed. I coolly continued staring at the computer screen. My inner voice was saying, "Why does this insolent little bastard think it's OK to intrude whenever he chooses? He needs a good ass-kicking. Yell at him now!"

He moved toward me, and the ninety-five-pound, gangly fourteen-year-old belligerently planted himself next to my computer chair. I said nothing. "I need help right now!" he insisted several times without pause. I waited. After about a minute, amid his relentless insistence, I picked up my phone and he asked what I was doing. "I'm calling your father," I said in a monotone. "I refuse to be treated like this, and you're going to have to leave." I had followed through on this threat on a prior occasion, so he knew I was serious. His face softened and he begged me not to do it. "Go upstairs," I told him, "and we'll see if we can work something out." Although from the outside I appeared as cool as a cucumber, inside I was burning up. I really wanted to let him have it. After he went upstairs, I went into the garage carrying two stress balls and squeezed them to release some of the built-up toxicity.

The irony of the situation is that Michael sings my praises to his teachers, psychologist, and psychiatrist. I have received at least a dozen referrals, thanks to him. "Kevin lets me be who I am," he told his father. "But when he gets mad, I don't take it personally." Although I am grateful for Michael's fondness of me, he is one of the most difficult children I have ever worked with. I have been successful with him due to a lot of hard work. In the first few months of working with Michael, I erupted at him several times. After such episodes, I felt like a fraud and a failure. I decided to take up the challenge and follow my own advice.

When I know Michael is coming over, I meditate for at least fifteen minutes beforehand. For me, meditation is a simple process in which I focus on my breath, watch thoughts and sensations, and then gently put my attention back on my breath. I have kept up this practice for so many years that I now do it all the time. It is not something that requires sitting on a cushion with incense burning. The essence of meditation for me is to cultivate the ability to watch my reactions without getting trapped in them. When I explode with anger, I have been ensnared. ADHDers are master trappers. Meditation is an extrasensory perception that allows me to see the trap on the trail and then to choose to walk around it.

Another technique I employ is visualization. I envision possible encounters I might have with students and imagine healthy responses. I take an inventory of my interactions with kids. Every day there are interactions I wish I had done differently. I spend a few minutes and imagine possible alternatives, and then see myself using them. This helps to wire new responses into me.

Knowing when to ask for help is another great ally in my work. In Michael's case, I spent hours on the phone with parents of other kids with Asperger's syndrome I have worked with, trying to brainstorm strategies and responses. A strong support network goes a long way toward allowing me to respond instead of reacting. When dealing with difficult kids, no one should try to go it alone.

I was only able to maintain calm in the interaction I described earlier, because I had spent a lot of time preparing for it. I responded to Michael in that moment, but did not react. That was a cultivated and intentional choice. You cannot control another's behavior, but you can control how you respond. If your past responses have been mostly of a negative nature, then doing the opposite of that can help bring the situation back into harmony.

> *With repeated angry responses to your ADHD loved one's behavior, you develop "neural trip wires."[3] You lay down neurological pathways in your brain that increase the chances of doing the same thing the next time. This is why it is so difficult to change.*

NOTICE POSITIVES

When your mindset is "the world is falling apart," you approach every day from a crisis mode. You operate with an ever-present fear that something bad is going to happen. You have not succeeded in getting your child or loved one under control, and you have anxiety that the situation is only going to get worse. Your loved one's life is like a dam, and you spend all of your energy in surveillance, watching and waiting for a small hole to appear so that you can plug it up quickly. With your attention almost exclusively on alert for problems, it is difficult, if not impossible, to see the good things when they occur.

I understand this mentality well. Like many an ADHD individual, I have struggled my whole life with a constant, low-grade anxiety. I deal with it every day, and it seems especially potent when I sit down to write or think about future goals. For some reason, as my creative juices start to flow, fears of the future overwhelm me. The antidote for me is to focus on positives. Today as I sat down to work on this book, my mind started churning out financial worries. I kept going to Yahoo!'s finance page and refreshing the Dow Jones stock index. As each click saw the market go down, my mood darkened. I slowly settled into an emotionally paralyzed state. Although I am quite accustomed to such episodes, it sometimes takes a few hours for me to realize what is happening. Once I become aware, I have a few methods that reliably help me get back on track. As I mentioned above, I keep a gratitude notebook. I take it out and write down at least twenty good things that have happened in the last week, including positive ideas or thoughts. Here is a partial version of today's list:

1. I have a great house.

2. I live in a quiet, wooded area.

3. I am professionally in demand.

4. I got my first book published.

5. I love what I do for a living.

6. I have supportive friends.

7. I do not have a boss. (Nobody is the boss of me.)

8. It is so easy to find scientific articles with the Internet.

9. Easybib.com makes referencing sources so easy!

10. My assistant, Will, gladly does all the tasks that I hate.

11. I have an extended family of ADHDers.

12. My family has become quite close, and I really enjoy them.

13. I have had lots of great mentors.

14. My sinus headaches have been much better the last few years.

15. My mother is still in good health.

It is a simple method, but it works well. Today, for instance, I went from a negative malaise to being quite productive on this book. In a study of organ recipients, researchers found that patients who kept "gratitude journals" scored higher on "measures of mental health, general health, and vitality than those who kept only routine notes about their days."[4] Robert Emmons, a University of California–Davis professor who specializes in the study of gratitude, found that "increased feelings of gratitude can cause people's well-being and quality of life to improve."[5] I recommend a gratitude journal to everyone, especially those struggling to overcome negativity. I pull out the gratitude journal when I have a strong urge to play a computer game. For me, downward spirals of negativity often give way to addictive, cyber-oriented cravings.

Many people scoff at the simplicity of this technique, but before you judge, I implore you to try it out. When you make your list, keep it with you and refer to it throughout the day. Try this technique for at least a month, five days a week, before you judge its effectiveness. It can change your attitude and, thus, change your life!

GIVE UP CONTROL

Another tool that can radically transform your relationship with the ADHDer in your life is giving up control. We ADHDers defy attempts to control us in career, school, and life. We embody the scientific principal of entropy, which states that the universe moves from a state of order to a state of chaos. It makes sense that we elicit controlling impulses from our parents, partners, teachers, and colleagues. Our rooms, desks, cars, and paperwork are often a mess.

One of my roommates in college, Martin, was an engineering major. He delighted in telling everybody, "Kevin is an entropy machine." He was a good guy in many respects, but my style of living irked him. He didn't get mad, though. He approached me every couple of weeks with a new system of organization that he was sure would transform my life. I give him great credit for effort and remarkable persistence. For reasons still unknown to me, we were roommates for four whole semesters. He tried to get me to experiment with a variety of different systems that relied on boxes, hanging baskets, milk crates, color codes, small industrial shipping containers, labels, and a closet organizer that had a system of pulleys. Martin was a well-meaning genius who saw potential in me and wanted to help. I was often flabbergasted at the amount of effort he put into these systems.

He went on to become a specialist in Just-in-Time manufacturing and inventory systems. I guess I was his first guinea pig. "You are one of the most multitalented people I have ever met," he told me. "If we could get you organized, you could conquer the world." The trouble was that every time Martin came up with a new system for me, I felt an instinctual impulse to resist. If that little twinge of discomfort that I felt in my abdomen had been able to speak, it would have said, "Stop trying to control to me."

I have seen similar resistance to "being controlled" from my ADHD students and clients. For that reason, I step cautiously when suggesting change. They have had so many people thrust so many great ideas on them that their defense mechanisms are highly honed. One of the greatest lessons I learned about getting past resistance came from a young man who had been a student and then became my intern. After my students graduate from high school, some who go to local colleges end up becoming my interns. They help me with younger students and, in exchange, I continue to help them keep their lives on track.

Will, a twenty-two-year-old ADHDer, was one of my most effective interns. At six foot four and more than 450 pounds, he had an imposing physical presence. I called him "the Guard." I took great pleasure in yelling, "Guard!" when I needed his help with a misbehaving student. Uttering "Guard" was often enough to quickly change a student's behavior with no further action needed. Will also prepared snacks for students, timed study breaks, managed the computer network, and assisted in implementing study skills and strategies. He admitted that he loved the control he had over the students, but he did not readily accept any advice from me.

Although he performed admirably as an intern, he would continually register for college classes and then stop going to them four or five weeks into the semester. Another problem was his weight. In spite of repeated attempts at dieting, he could not shed any pounds and had become diabetic. I tried lecturing him into submission. I printed out articles about the ravaging impact of obesity. I gave him daily pep talks about how talented he was and how I appreciated having him around. I tried getting him to talk about his classes, but he allowed no discussion. All of my words went in one ear and out the other. He effortlessly tuned everything out and did not even seem bothered. I had to change tactics.

"Will," I said, "I'm starting to put on weight, but I have trouble making it to the gym." He quickly offered, "Maybe you should find a workout partner." Even though Will rarely accepts advice, he is quick to offer it to others. I asked, "How about if you were my workout partner? That way, you could make sure I went." He responded, "I don't have the money for a gym membership." I trumped this evasive maneuver by offering to pay for his membership as long as he went three times a week with me. I figured I was getting off cheaply; the membership was, after all, only forty dollars a month.

"You have to make sure I go," I told him. "I don't want to end up with a bulging belly like my older brother has." Will had very little self-discipline, but he delighted in enforcing rules and commitments with others. A few weeks into our arrangement, I told him, "I don't feel like going today." He eagerly challenged my apathy: "You told me to do whatever it takes to get you to the gym. So I've taken the liberty of hiding your cell phone and changing the password on your laptop. Are you driving, or shall I?" I was able to get Will to start exercising by giving him control over an aspect of my life I was having trouble with. He actually started losing weight because he exercised, too, recording a 125-pound weight loss in one year. He no longer works for me, but we have continued our mutually beneficial arrangement.

Will taught me that control is often not the answer to resistance. Giving up control, on the other hand, can pay great dividends. I am constantly on the lookout with my students for unique ways they can help me. Fifteen-year-old Ryan is highly attuned to others' emotions. I take him into my confidence on a regular basis and ask his opinion about other students. I even ask him to critique my handling of situations. He never fails to give honest—sometimes hard-to-hear—feedback. The more I ask for his opinions, the more he ends up asking for mine. Drew, on the other hand, is not the greatest judge of character but is exceptionally mechanically inclined. I bemoan my own lack of mechanical inclination (which is the truth) when I talk to him, giving him a way to be superior to me. Last year, when there was a three-day power outage, I called Drew and told him my generator would not start. He couldn't wait to come over and help me. It took him about three minutes to get the thing going. Ever since that day, Drew has been much more willing to accept advice from me regarding school. He has gone from a 1.5 grade point average to a 3.3. He loves telling the story about how he restored power to my house!

Letting go of control is the opposite of how most people would instinctually respond to an ADHDer. If you find ways of giving up control, you may be able to bypass what often feels like a fortress of resistance. Find strengths in your ADHDer, and then figure out how he or she could use those strengths to legitimately help you. There can be no greater boost to that person's self-esteem!

THE LAWS OF PHYSICS

Newton's third law states, "For every action, there is an equal and opposite reaction." This law applies to force and motion. Most parents apply the logic of this principle to their children, and to good effect. Children need boundaries to be set and consistently maintained. Bad behavior should be met with predictable consequences, and good behavior should be rewarded. ADHD individuals also need consistent and responsible parenting. We ADHDers do not always behave in ways that others consider logical and reasonable, however, so dealing with us often requires a slight modification to Newton's principle: For every reaction you have, there is always an equal and opposite reaction. Find the opposite and you may unlock the key to effectively dealing with the ADHDer in your life.

CHAPTER 5

HUMOR, CLASS CLOWNS, AND WILLIAM SHAKESPEARE

"Humor is mankind's greatest blessing."
Mark Twain

ACADEMIC ESPIONAGE

As a grade-school boy—and I still struggle with this in my forties—I found keeping track of papers and assignments a daunting task. If I had done the work, why was it so important that it get turned in? Wasn't my word good enough for the teacher? "She knows I am a bright kid," I would reason to myself. "She should just give me an A and leave me alone. Why all this fuss about actually *giving* her the paper?" I felt misunderstood. I knew what I had done and what I was capable of. Why wasn't that enough?

I also believed I was smart and struggled to understand why my grades were not higher. I would anxiously ask myself, "Why aren't I getting all As? Everybody tells me how smart I am. Don't smart people deserve As?" The situation confused me. The work was easy, but all those mimeographed sheets with purple ink (which I admit I enjoyed sniffing) overwhelmed me, as did the incessant cutting, pasting, and craft-oriented projects. Paper-bag turkey puppets with orange construction-paper feathers? What were we supposed to learn from that in the fourth grade? The amount of busy work was staggering, and so painfully dull.

I tried to care. I tried to give it my best effort, but most of the stuff we did was so wrong from my perspective. The whole school thing felt like torture, or a prison, with Sister Raphael as the warden. If I close my eyes I can feel the mind-numbing stupor I was in most of the school day. Thank God I had a reservoir for my frustration, otherwise it would have spilled out all the time.

When school got out I used to run my fastest all the way home. I think this was one of the unconscious methods I used to discharge the frustration. That run home from school was often interrupted by a prank or some act of petty vandalism, like turning on "Old Lady" Schumacher's hose and letting it run, opening a gate and letting out someone's dog to roam free, or simply ringing someone's doorbell and scampering away before he or she answered. These were all acts of a frustrated child, and it's pretty clear to me that school was the main source of that frustration. This feeling was compounded by all the adults outside of school telling me how smart I was, making my failure to perform especially difficult to bear.

The ADHD teens that attend my ADHD Study Groups are usually worn down. By the time they come to me, most have accepted as fact that they will never do well in school. School is a cauldron of incessant negativity that does not value their gifts and perceptual preferences. It's of critical importance, therefore, that families affirm their ADHD loved ones.

There is no monolithic ADHD. ADHD is, in many respects, a catch-all term that describes a lot of different personality and behavioral profiles.[1] The one constant with ADHD is that there *are* no constants. However, I have seen in myself and the ADHDers with whom I have worked an uncommonly high inclination to humor. It is just a part of who we effortlessly are.

Some of us make life exciting through our natural inclinations to interrupt routines and ignore expectations. Since we constantly look for novelty and excitement to stimulate our underactive brains, and are typically more than eager to share our findings with others, we provide the world—when it pays attention—with a natural antidote to boredom. Even those lower-energy and primarily inattentive ADHDers among us have a heightened appreciation for comedy. My students and clients of this type are often Internet mavens who search and scan for funny videos and jokes to pass along to others.

This innate penchant for humor is among the great gifts we have offered humanity over the millennia. Many people who come into regular contact with us complain that we are just too intense, too prone to pushing the limits and crossing the boundaries. Humor is often where the limits and boundaries of society are first broached and expanded. The jokes that once landed Lenny Bruce in jail are now considered suitable for late-night television. Societal taboos are regular fodder for stand-up comedians, whose treatment of such issues becomes the talk of the whole country. Not all stand-up comedians have ADHD, but as a comedian and ADHD coach, I can tell you that a high percentage do. People do not generally go into stand-up comedy because they enjoy routine, stability, and predictability. It is an incredibly difficult business fraught with rejection, roadblocks, and a high degree of intensity. Without ADHDers, there would be far fewer comedians and far less laughter in the world.

EXCITING OR ANNOYING?

Although medication and behavioral modification strategies can make life easier for us, the genius—and sometimes giftedness—of being ADHD receives incredibly short shrift. We dare to try new things. We possess irrepressible courage to explore, even to the point of exposing ourselves to danger. Comedic interpretation of life runs naturally through our veins. ADHD may make certain aspects of life challenging, but it also allows us to contribute in unique and extraordinary ways.

We can make life difficult for teachers and coworkers because we abhor sitting in one place for a long time and doing monotonous tasks. The mundane and the routine do not engage ADHDers. We naturally gravitate, therefore, toward the novel and the unusual, and some of us even have variants of genes that seem to predispose us to novelty-seeking behavior.[2]

> *Many of the drugs that work well in ADHD people have an impact on the brain's dopamine pathways. Dopamine is a neurotransmitter that is involved in the reward circuitry of the brain, but more specifically, it is about survival. Dopamine plays a key role in motivation, which is often impaired in ADHDers. A variant of the dopamine receptor gene DRD4, found in 29 percent of ADHDers, has been associated with greater impulsivity and hyperactivity.[3] The way that the dopamine system works in ADHDers means that we have an atypical way of motivating ourselves, often needing much more intensity than the average person. Many ADHD people keep themselves focused and motivated in "boring" situations through the use of humor. It is important to keep in mind that ADHD is a condition governed by the neurobiological environment of the brain.*

The novelty seeking that many ADHDers exhibit explains why so many of us are skateboarders, daredevils, and bungee-jumpers. We are an economic pillar of stability for the nation's emergency rooms. Almost single-handedly, we keep them humming along with newly traumatized patients. But not all who possess this predisposition are physical risk-takers. Many seek novelty and excitement in academic pursuits, entrepreneurship, and even stand-up comedy.

EXPLORING NEW LANDS

Who but an ADHDer would have thought it a good idea to cross an ocean that terrified almost everyone on the European continent?

Christopher Columbus proved to be a dogged and tireless explorer, but once his job turned from perilous adventurer to sedentary governor, he was forced to stay and perform perfunctory and repetitious duties. In exploration-discovery mode, all of Columbus's internal resources were singularly trained on an adventure, a state of being that allowed him to overcome many obstacles. His performance in the tasks of building a colony, however, so displeased King Ferdinand and Queen Isabella that he was eventually taken back to Spain in chains and stripped of his noble titles. Columbus naturally exhibited the energy of the proverbial hunter, excelling under the pressure and intensity of the chase.[4] He, like many a hunter, was at home amid such crises as dealing with mutiny and the ever-looming possibility of death.

Columbus's tragic demise parallels what happens to many ADHDers: We exhibit phenomenal performance when we find an assignment engaging, but mundane tasks leave us in the dust. Our natural talents often go to waste. Our enormous reservoirs of energy frequently have no outlet, so we can be a source of disruption and disharmony in enterprises for which we are not well suited: classroom lectures, deskbound office environments, and long meetings in which the same points are reiterated ad infinitum. Such situations madden us.

ADHDers are brilliant at breaking up monotony, and they suffer greatly when shackled to tedium and repetition. Most of us ADHDers experience the world as a place that does not honor our natural gifts and adds insult to injury by labeling us defective. We may internalize the scorn that is heaped upon us by parents, friends, work, and school, making it easier for society to relegate us to the sidelines.

COURT JESTER

William Shakespeare, by contrast, did our kind great service in his multiple portrayals of the archetypal fool: the court jester. Many an ADHD youth naturally gravitates toward this role in school. As Shakespeare himself wrote in *As You Like It*, "a fool thinks himself to be wise, but a wise man knows himself to be a fool." For Shakespeare, to have a fool attending you is generally a mark of distinction. It suggests the possibility of redemption, of possessing enough flexibility and openness to change one's path. To employ a fool is usually an indication that one is—potentially at least—wise.[5] The term "fool" is misleading because of its suggestion of stupidity or a lack of common sense. (Many ADHDers find themselves weighed down with such labels early in their school careers.) Quite the contrary, the court jester—or fool— played a very important role in court life. Rulers in many European courts permitted the fool to blurt out whatever came to mind, to question commonly held assumptions, and even to ridicule excesses and inconsistencies. (If only classroom teachers valued those behaviors!) The jester shadowed the king, constantly scanning the verbal exchanges of court life, and—by engaging a supremely divergent mind—arrived at fresh interpretations. Whereas monarchs and their various chamberlains, courtiers, and advisors attempted to "stay on task" to resolve problems and forge decisions, the jester's role was to offer balance through unorthodox perspectives and original thinking.

Shakespeare uses both King Lear's fool and Feste, from *Twelfth Night*, to expose human folly and to show monarchs and nobility their true motives while pointing out unpleasant realities that other members of the court were too sheepish to mention. In *Twelfth Night*, Olivia alludes to the skill and value of the fool when she declares, "This fellow is wise enough to play the fool." King Lear's fool, like his own daughter Cordelia, is a truth-teller.[6] In spite of Lear's threat to have the fool whipped, the fool continues taunting his master with unpleasant truths that Lear would rather not think about. In *As You Like It*, the fool, Touchstone, creates an impression simply by his name. Geologists and prospectors employ touchstones to test precious metals. Court jesters provided rulers with a different type of touchstone, a reliable sounding board to help them discover their own internal gold and root it out from the slag.

Like the German folk hero Till Eulenspiegel ("Eule" in German means owl, obviously associated with wisdom, and "spiegel" means mirror), jesters hold up a mirror and let us see our own ugliness and shortcomings, often using humor to remove some of the emotional sting of unpleasant revelations. Jesters and fools have stood as a check to the tendency of human societies throughout history to enforce conformity. For much of recorded history, the jester's voice has offered alternatives by questioning cultural assumptions. Many of us ADHDers are the spiritual descendants of these noble individuals. We likewise exhibit a remarkable penchant for one of the jester's primary tools: humor!

A proficient jester has the ability to convey hard-to-admit truths with laughter. Psychological research suggests that people exhibit greater openness to new data when humor accompanies the information.[7] Court jesters have had instinctual awareness of this wisdom for millennia. It should, of course, come as no shock that ADHDers, like jesters, exhibit uncommon giftedness in the comedic arts. We just don't cognitively process in the same way most others do, so we're forever venturing outside the box.

When we think of performing outside of the box, improvisation comes to mind. This often-misunderstood art form involves the skill of quickly scanning diverse associations and picking one that will defeat, or counteract, the expectations of the audience. Incongruity, when an idea or object is out of place, is the most basic essence of humor.[8] Well, we ADHDers love to quickly scan, and we get an enormous kick from pointing out incongruity (mental health professionals call this "distractibility" and teachers call it "smart-aleck behavior"). That's why we don't pay attention to teachers when they talk *at* us. Likewise, we're often the first ones to notice a bird in a tree or a deer off in the distance when we're walking through the woods. We don't consciously try, but rather this constant scanning trait seems to be hardwired into us.

Rapid mental scanning is only one of the aptitudes needed for a comedic performer. A mind finely tuned to subtle associations is another. The ADHD mind is like setting off on a trip without an itinerary or a fixed plan. The joyous anticipation of the excursion comes from the possibility of finding something new. Divergence, venturing "off the beaten path," is welcomed and embraced. Convergent thinking, the opposite of the above approach, would be akin to mapping out the route in advance and sticking rigidly to the plan. This style lends itself to efficiency but not to exploration, and it does not provide nearly as much fun and excitement.

Openness to new possibilities stands as one of the essential elements of comedy, as many comedic writers have pointed out. From this openness, it's easier to uncover an association that is contrary to what might be expected.[9] "The setup line of a joke creates a first story . . . that leads us to expect something, then the punch line surprises us with a second story that is different from what we're expecting."[10]

Comedian Tom Naughton has done excellent work researching the core of humor, as well as the joke structures that reliably make people laugh. During my study of Naughton's work, I had a "Eureka!" moment. It dawned on me why the ADHD mind was so often adept at joke creation. One of Naughton's categories, Mix and Match, will illustrate the point.[11] Comedians employ Mix and Match by pairing together two disparate pieces of information (a skill at which ADHDers often excel magnificently). The first bit of information, the *setup*, creates an expectation that the second piece of information subsequently shatters.

A classic Rodney Dangerfield joke exemplifies this technique: "I get no respect. I was crossing the street. . . . I got hit by the Bookmobile. I'm lying there screaming; the guy looks at me and says, 'Shh!'"

DELIGHT IN DISPARITY

An ADHDer in the classroom, or in a meeting at work, often takes more delight from shattering people's realities than from participating in them. Most people take this sort of behavior as an insult. It is merely a function, however, of how our creative and exploratory minds work. When an ADHDer receives new information or is in a new situation, the mind naturally and automatically brings a freshness that underlies the ability to glean new insights and perspectives.

Another joke will illustrate a feature of our humorous abilities in which we take particular delight: defeating expectations. (By contrast, we often feel defeated by our frequent inability to live up to the expectations that others thrust upon us!) If I say, "I took my father out for Thanksgiving,"[12] you will probably have an automatic—perhaps completely unconscious—expectation of what that means. Obviously, I took my father out for a meal. The line is structured to lead you to that conclusion. Thanksgiving is, after all, associated with eating. Playing on that reality, an adept comedian will deliver a punch line that destroys the picture that you have created for yourself. Your own biases and beliefs determine the way that you perceive the information.

One of the jobs of the comedian is to flip that perception. To shatter the picture of taking my father out for dinner, I could follow up by saying, "That old bastard deserved it." Or I could deliver the message with "That was the best ten thousand bucks I ever spent." Your old picture is gone now, and in its place is a new reality that reveals an unexpected meaning of the original statement. You now know that I had my father killed. I've always wanted to be on *America's Most Wanted*, so here's my chance.

The bottom line here is that we ADHDers are good at making people laugh because our natural style of thinking lends itself to making unexpected associations between seemingly unrelated pieces of data. This simple—yet hard-to-master—method underpins the fundamental structure of comedy.

THE BANE OF YOUR EXISTENCE

For a classroom teacher, a student's tendency to bring up divergent associations can be difficult to bear. The night before a lesson, good teachers figure out what it is they want to communicate to students the next day, and great teachers develop methods to allow the students to fully participate in their learning. Most teachers pride themselves on keeping the class "on task," which can be a challenge when an ADHDer is afoot. Picture this scenario: the bell rings and the history teacher quiets down the class. He plods right into his lesson with a serious and staccato tone designed to transmit to the students the gravity of General Washington's predicament: "It was bitterly cold that early December morning in 1776, when George Washington took his troops in boats across the frozen Delaware River. The General, however, inspired confidence and . . . What, Kevin?"

"Mr. DeLuca?" I ask earnestly. "Why did they cross the river in boats if it was frozen? Couldn't they just walk across, or were they worried about the ice breaking?"[13]

"Well, I'm not sure that the river itself was frozen, Kevin, but at least it was very cold out," Mr. DeLuca dutifully informs me, somewhat encouraged by the fact that I seem engaged in the subject matter.

"Were there, like, pieces of ice floating around?" I inquisitively follow up. "Or were there, like, little icebergs that they had to watch out for?"

"Uh, I'm not totally sure," Mr. DeLuca responds, starting to get annoyed, "but maybe there were pieces of ice. Anyway . . ." Mr. DeLuca says with staggered intonation to signal the end of the discussion, "when Washington and his ragged troops arrived on the other side . . . Do you have another question, Kevin?" the teacher inquires with impatience.

"Yeah, but since they had small boats, those pieces of ice could have smashed into them and sank them, just like what happened to the *Titanic*," I plaintively insist, undeterred by the teacher's attempt to *stay on task*. "Since they didn't have Polident back then," I seriously posit, "why weren't Washington's false teeth chattering?"

"OK, Kevin, out!" Mr. DeLuca demands.

"What did I do?" I ask innocently.

It may seem that I was deliberately trying to derail the lecture. My mind was simply questioning an incongruity in the story, perhaps even disdaining the official version. I made unlikely associations, followed my fancy, and took a divergent path of learning.

The other students laughed at this point, but I had not asked my questions to make them laugh. I simply followed my inquisitive mind down seemingly divergent paths—I have found that this often makes others laugh. The incongruity between American History and clattering dentures induced my fellow students to crack up. I had no clue that I was barraging Mr. DeLuca with silly questions, nor was I fully aware of the disruption it caused. I was just being me, and I had not yet learned that speaking my mind often created problems. Incidentally, I remember that lecture like it was yesterday, probably because I fully participated.

What I needed was a manual on how my brain worked and what the consequences of my hardwiring were likely to be. I desperately needed someone to teach me that I had gifts that could be powerfully exploited. Instead, from an early age I was bombarded with criticism and what seemed to me to be frequent assaults on my character. My early adult life was consequently spent dealing with deep issues of shame and inadequacy, and try-ing to ascertain where those feelings came from.

Whether you're an ADHDer, a parent, a professional, or just a curious soul, I want to reiterate that the differences that charac-terize the ADHD mind also hold the potential for remarkable ap-titudes and achievement. If you look carefully, underneath every ADHD "symptom," you will uncover a gift. The gift of laughter stands out as one of the most precious.

PLAY AS NECESSITY

"Work before you play" is a maxim most people would agree with. It certainly underpins the work ethic of the Western world.[14] But for ADHDers, this type of logic does not work very well. Play, excitement, and humor energize us, making us more powered-up to then tackle work that needs to be done. Lack of these things, on the other hand, drains us. Fun teachers get surprisingly high levels of productivity out of ADHDers, while those on the serious side of the teaching spectrum put us to sleep or "inspire" us to cause trouble.

When parents bring ADHDers to one of my Study Groups, the students usually come kicking and screaming. They assume—since they are coming to work on school-related matters—that the boredom and frustration of school will naturally follow. During the last thirteen years, I have taken great pains to make sure that never happens!

I often begin my initial session, which parents and student attend, by discussing what things the young person does for fun. Most often, we have activities and interests in common, so I spend five to ten minutes discussing those. I do not do this half-heartedly; instead, I fully engage because having fun is the most important thing for me too. I succeeded in school only because I made a game out of it. The students and I discuss skiing, paint-ball, airsoft guns, skateboarding, favorite comedians, movies, and—most often—favorite video games, a topic that often leads to me showing them my book on the subject. I tell them, "You might wonder how an ADHDer like me could write a whole book. The trick was making the whole process fun, and that's what my Study Groups aim to help you do with school."

They are shocked during their first official session, because I usually only let them work for about twenty minutes and then insist they stop for a quick video game break. I have the Xbox, Nintendo 64, and two big-screen TVs. We have video game tournaments every couple of weeks. Whoever can beat Alex, my video game–crazed intern, in *Mario Kart* or *Super Smash Bros.* gets a free Slurpee! I also have puzzle games like Jenga and Rubik's Cube on the tables. Many ADHDers need to use their hands; they are tactile and, more often than not, hands-on learners. Sundays after 7 p.m. are game nights; we play Monopoly, Apples to Apples, Risk, and many others. Playing games with others is a great way to improve social skills as well!

I have come to believe that if I let ADHD folks be themselves, fun and excitement will surely follow. I like to say that Study Groups create an ADHD-affirmative environment. Not only do we have serious fun, but we take fun seriously. I have a comedy notebook in the main study room, and whenever someone comes up with a good joke, sight gag, or impersonation, we write in the notebook. Humor is treated as a precious asset. It is honored and appreciated. Learn to value humor with the ADHDer in your life, and your relationship with him or her will likely improve.

You will find no better tool to interact with an ADHDer than having fun. The interaction will energize and build rapport in a way that you never imagined. Self-help guru Wayne Dyer says that "every problem has a spiritual solution." With an ADHDer, almost every problem can be solved with fun. If you keep that in mind, you can revolutionize the relationship with your ADHDer, and you may help him or her succeed in ways that were previously unimaginable. As you seek to come up with new strategies to help your ADHD loved one succeed, remember that fun, humor, and excitement are catalysts that will make the process much more effective.

COMPASSIONATE COMEDIAN

Tony Vicich has been has been taking comedy seriously for three decades. Tony is a highly reflective individual who has struggled with ADHD, and in this, as with all his struggles, he has incredible passion for helping others avoid his own pitfalls and mistakes. He battled substance abuse in his early adult life but has been clean and sober for more than twenty years. Because he is active in Twelve Step circles in Los Angeles, many people refer to him as the "AA sponsor to the stars." He has helped a large number of famous people beat substance abuse.

Tony is a veteran stand-up comedian who has been featured on numerous television programs, including *Evening at the Improv* as well as Showtime, MTV, and Comedy Central specials. I met him more than ten years ago as I started following my dream of becoming a stand-up comedian. I attended his comedy workshops and worked with him one-on-one for several years. When my brand of comedy was not playing well in bars and clubs, he helped launch me on a new path. As I wallowed in self-pity and failure, Tony insightfully helped me uncover where my talents truly lay. "Look, you're going to nightclubs where people want jokes about sex, substance abuse, and stupidity," he said. "That's not you. I see you more as a writer, putting together a one-man show about your life and work, or maybe even writing books." I took Tony's advice, and here I am. Sometimes we need a charismatic mentor to see into us and get us to accept and own the truth of who we really are. Tony has done that for scores of stand-up comics, ADHDers, and substance abusers, many of whom are all three at once.

Tony's wisdom regarding his own path underpins the support he gives to others. "When people ask me why I got hooked on alcohol and drugs," Tony said, "I tell them there are no easy answers. Suffice it to say that I have always had this need for excitement, and I didn't find positive ways to get it met." Possessing a superior IQ, Tony was always bored in school and frequently got in trouble. "I didn't see the point, and a whole string of nuns, priests, and teachers couldn't get me to the see the point," Tony said. "But when you don't do well in school, you take on negative messages about yourself. Substance abuse allowed me, for a time, to ignore those messages, and life sure had a lot more drama with booze and drugs in it." Tony remained certain throughout his school years of his own intelligence and abilities, however. His family helped affirm his gifts. "My mother and brother never stopped believing in me," he said. "They delighted in my humor and made me feel I was special."

Immediately after high school, Tony uprooted and went to Los Angeles. "I felt fully alive when I got to L.A.," Tony said. "It was like the scene vibrated at the same frequency I was on, a frequency that was definitely not OK in school." He enrolled in method acting classes, following principles formulated by Lee Strasberg. Although he enjoyed acting, stand-up comedy felt like a better fit. "When I was onstage in a club," Tony said, "it was like I was doing school all over, only I was in charge and everybody was interested and had a good time. It was a life-affirming experience." Tony toured the country for more than a decade, but that lifestyle took its toll on his family. "I decided my daughter needed a full-time father and that her well-being was more important than my pursuit of wealth and fame," Tony said. He remained in the comedy business as a nightclub owner, promoter, teacher, and coach. He has devoted his life to helping younger comedians obtain success.

Tony has also used comedy to help ADHDers. He and I offer a workshop called "ADHD for Fun," which inspired me to write this book. We help ADHD teens see comedy as a tool and an asset to be honed and practiced. "So often, ADHD children are labeled 'class clown,' 'smart aleck,' and 'wise guy,'" Tony said. "At our workshop, we teach them that they have valuable skills that can be used to achieve success in school, career, and life. These humor-oriented young people often possess amazing creativity. They can use that to come up with creative methods to succeed in areas they may find boring. We focus on strengths and how to use them."

Tony has some advice for parents, teachers, and professionals: "We have to be careful that we don't put creative people into straitjackets of conformity. We live in a world that, in many ways, teeters on the brink of disaster. The creativity so common among ADHDers is something this planet desperately needs. Amid the fear that seems to grip the world right now, we also need the humor and joy that ADHD people effortlessly bring."

HUMOR TO THE FRONT LINE

Scientific research suggests that Tony is onto something. Humor takes the sting out of frustration, can lessen conflict,[15] and has a proven therapeutic benefit. By contrast, many scientific studies show that people whose anger is not abated by humor have a much higher risk of heart attack or the need for a secondary angioplasty.[16] Depressed people have significantly higher medical costs.[17] One study that looked more carefully at the physiological impact of humor assessed participants while they watched stress-producing films and again while they watched comedies. During periods of laughter, blood flow to endothelial cells, a key component in cardiovascular health, increased 22 percent, while decreasing 35 percent during stress, making the net difference between blood flow during stress and blood flow during laughter more than 50 percent.[18] Children ages 7 to 16 had greater tolerance for pain when watching funny videos during a standardized pain task—like placing a hand in cold water—than when viewing the videos right before or after the task.[19] Humor has powerful benefits.

If you have an ADHDer in your life, arm yourself with humor. Find funny videos online. Watch, share, and talk about them with your ADHDer. If you see a funny comic strip in the paper, cut it out and post it on the refrigerator. If your ADHD loved one says or does something funny, write it down. Bring it up to him or her later, and tell other people. Watch funny TV shows with your loved one, or even go out to a comedy club together. Make laughter and humor major priorities. Take humor seriously.

CHAPTER 6

THE TOOL CHEST: SUCCESS IN SCHOOL AND LIFE

"When the only tool you own is a hammer,
every problem begins to resemble a nail."
Abraham Maslow, founder of humanistic psychology

I have developed a tool chest that offers specific strategies for completing tasks in an ADHD-friendly manner. If you have ADHD, this chapter will help you help yourself, as well as provide insight into better understanding of the people in your life who do not have ADHD. If you are the parent or spouse of an ADHDer, this chapter will assist you in becoming a more effective helper, arming you at the very least with a new mindset. It will also give you a window into the details of my personal and professional experience. The pages that follow are not as much a step-by-step blueprint for change as they are a guide to infusing tasks with creativity, movement, and play. Once you start thinking of tasks and responsibilities through the lens of "The Opposite," the possibilities are endless.

The majority of folks I work with are middle school, high school, and college students, but I have also used the methods in this chapter with students in medical and law schools, people preparing for the GRE, and businesspeople wanting to advance professionally. Although the lessons that follow focus on academics, they are also applicable to life and career.

THE VICTIM MENTALITY

ADHDers often have a victim complex. There is a reason for this. We certainly are "victims" of DNA. We have been hardwired differently, making it difficult to fit in. We did not choose this. The trouble is that victims spend their time justifying a lack of fulfillment, time that could just as easily be spent taking steps toward success.

Victimhood is a refuge from repeated failure. One of the greatest challenges I regularly face is convincing ADHDers that despite multiple past failures, they can still succeed. Constant gloom gives a measure of protection from the sting of failure. It is less painful to stay mired in negativity than it is to muster enough hope to try again. The simple act of hoping risks yet another defeat, which leads to greater despair. My ADHD students and clients ward off my encouragement with dark clouds of resignation:

- "Why should I try? I'm never going to do well in that class."

- "I hate my life, and it's never going to get better."

- "Why do bad things always happen to me?"

- "What did I do to deserve this?"

- "I'm stupid, and that's not going to change."

- "The teacher doesn't like me."

- "Nobody likes me."

With some students, the negativity is so thick that it rubs off on me. I presently have one fifteen-year-old student, Rachel, who is so powerfully pessimistic that she can bring down five, six, or even seven other students during Study Groups. "I'm so stupid, and it's only going to get worse," she said as she struggled with algebra. It's not so much what she says, but the densely packed, depressive malaise that she exudes. My only weapon against her onslaught of negativity is humor. "Oh, that's good!" I told her, as though I were a film director. "Can you dig down and really bring up some self-hatred? I know there's more." Luckily, she usually laughs and lightens up when I get playful with her. It's all I can do to keep from being dragged down. (By the way, playful connection helps many ADHDers come out of despair.)[1]

I find that pep talks usually won't accomplish much. Rachel needed new tools, not more words. One reason she was so negative was that she had an above-average IQ but a 1.7 grade point average. She tried to do well, but she never managed to put all the pieces together. As I delved into the details with Rachel, I found that she generally studied by sitting in her room for long periods of time with the textbook open. She readily admitted that her mind wandered and that she simply read the book over and over. It never dawned on Rachel that there was more than one way to study. For one biology test, she calculated that she had spent seven hours preparing. She got a D. "I felt like an idiot," she said. "I put all that time in and almost failed." When I finally convinced her that the right techniques could cut her study time in half and get better results, she was willing to try some different methods. As with every ADHD client, I had to help her to tease out her personal goals. Goals are the engine of change.

Tool #1: Setting Goals

ADHDers have great difficulty figuring out their goals, partly because they spend so much of their energy resisting goals that other people impose on them. We set our minds on what we do not want and too often neglect what we actually want. Daniel Amen believes that having goals helps create an "auxiliary prefrontal cortex."[2] In other words, reminding oneself of goals every day helps stimulate the underactive part of the ADHD brain.

Executive functions *can be defined as "neurocognitive processes that maintain an appropriate problem-solving set to attain a later goal."[3] Although understanding is still somewhat limited, scientists concur that executive functions are generally controlled by the prefrontal areas of the brain.[4] Numerous neuroimaging studies show that these parts of the brain demonstrate altered structure and irregular patterns of activity in ADHD.[5] The main thing to keep in mind is that ADHD derives not from individual will, but from neurobiological differences.*

Here is a list of long-term and short-term goals that can get the process started. It is important to have a grand vision for our lives, while at the same time thinking through the small things we can do every day to achieve them. To initiate the goal-setting process, a few questions can be beneficial. Each question implies a series of goals.

Is there anybody you argue with a lot?

- Possible long-term goal: Stop arguing.

- Possible short-term goal: No arguments Monday, Wednesday, Friday.

Do you like school?

- Possible long-term goal: Enjoy school more.

- Possible short-term goals: Brainstorm things I like about school, find ways to interact playfully with teachers, try to get teachers I know I will like.

Are you happy with your grades?

- Possible long-term goal: 3.3 grade point average.

- Possible short-term goals: Develop a creative study plan, go to school early and meet with teachers three days a week, find and practice with online quizzes, make up my own practice tests and take them, study on the treadmill.

Do you like your job?

- Possible long-term goal: Enjoy work more (put energy into making myself more attractive to other possible employers).

- Possible short-term goals: Set up my work area in a way that pleases me, go to lunch with people I like, stop complaining and focus on the good things about work, find a way to make my job more creative.

Do you have all the money you want?

- Possible long-term goal: Have more money by cutting expenses.

- Possible short-term goals: Use my cell phone less and cut back my plan, drive in a way that maximizes fuel economy, eat out less, unplug electronic devices when not in use, develop a monthly budget.

The possibilities are endless. Once big goals come to mind, it is important to break them down into baby steps. The Japanese have a system called "Kaizen" that they use for continuous improvement. The idea of Kaizen is that small, perhaps imperceptible, steps taken each day lead to huge changes over time. Again, it is crucial to think through as many baby steps as possible so that some small success can be achieved every day.

It is useful to make up a Microsoft Word document in a large font that contains all long-term and short-term goals. These can be printed and placed on a bedroom wall, in the car, or on a bathroom mirror. The refrigerator will work, too, but for teenagers it is prudent to place this sheet in an area where friends won't see it. I have had clients abandon this method because of teasing. Teenagers are hypersensitive to the opinions of their peers.

With ADHDers, a combination of different strategies always works best. What works for one individual may not work for another, and what works well one week may not continue to be of benefit. Hava, an adult ADHD coaching client, has found a routine that she keeps in place through a support network. She takes twenty minutes or so every Sunday night to make goal sheets for each day of the coming week. She e-mails her goals to me, and then we follow up with our weekly coaching call, during which I offer feedback. "I put check boxes next to each item," she told me, "because when I complete a task and check it off, it helps energize me for the next thing." Here's an example:

Monday, May 3

☐ 1. Make up a grocery list

☐ 2. Go grocery shopping

☐ 3. Put groceries away PROPERLY

☐ 4. Fill out soccer camp paperwork for Josh

☐ 5. Sign up Melissa for summer swimming

☐ 6. Return Simon and Garfunkel tickets by MAY 12!!!

☐ 7. Research venues for Sandy's shower

Hava told me recently, "This system works for me. Some days I resist following it. When that happens, I call in the troops: my ADHD coach, friends, and sometimes even my husband." Support and connection with others are crucial for achieving goals!

Along with posting goals, it can very useful to display pictures of people who have a life that you want for yourself. You can search the Internet, Facebook, and even family photo albums. It is important to aim high, but it is equally important to ensure that you pick someone whose lifestyle you could actually attain. You can place the photos in your car or on your walls, or even set them as your computer background. One of my adult ADHD clients created a lengthy list of people, got a picture for each person, and then made up two poster boards with a collage on each. She put one in her bedroom and one in the kitchen and made sure to look at them every day. Notice how her list contains family members, famous people, and general categories of people:

1. My aunt Marcie

2. My mom

3. My husband Sol

4. People who complete what they start out to accomplish

5. Dave Marcus

6. My dad

7. Kevin Roberts

8. Randi Krupicki

9. Anyone who holds down a job

10. My personal trainer Nancy

11. Shana Friedman

12. People who have balance in their lives

13. People who work out regularly and consistently

14. People who are fit

15. Noah (our son) because of his lust for life, learning, and excitement with new experiences. (Plus he has more concentration than me, and he is only three and a half!!)

16. Maya Angelou

17. Kahlil Gibran

For the general categories, she found pictures on the Internet. She said, "I'm very visual, so seeing the collages of photos every day gets in my brain and motivates me. Sometimes I take one of them in the car, almost like I have the people with me as I go about my day."

Goals and visual reminders of them are powerful. As an additional measure, I program goal reminders into my cell phone at random times. Today at 10 a.m., for example, I was reminded, "Finish chapter 6." That's what I'm doing at the moment.

It may be necessary to find a coach, therapist, or support group (e.g., CHADD) to help with goals. People often have little success helping their ADHD loved ones identify and implement goals. One of the greatest pitfalls is failing to celebrate small victories. Whenever some small goal is achieved, recognize it and find a way to celebrate.

Tool #2: Assume the Worst

We have already covered lists in terms of goal setting, but listing can be useful in a variety of ways. We ADHDers miss details. The only way I have a prayer of keeping commitments and responsibilities is to regularly assume that I have forgotten something. I brainstorm and write down whatever comes to mind.

Within five minutes of a student's arrival at one of my ADHD Study Groups, I sit down with him or her to make a list of homework that needs to get done and inquire about possible upcoming tests. I keep track of this information on a note card so that I can check in with the student periodically throughout the time he or she is at group. After a few months, I have students start doing this for themselves. Invariably, we run into difficulties.

Students may declare, "I don't have that much to do today" or "I already did all my homework." This is the kind of thinking that gets them into trouble, so I must confront them. There are many questions we can ask to get at the truth:

- Did you check the teacher's website?
- Did you talk to anyone else in the class to make sure you're right?
- Did you fill in your planner?
- If there were homework, what might it be?
- If you were the teacher, what would you have told the students to do?

In these moments, it is useful to recall the classes in which that student has missed assignments before. In many cases, this can be verified by visiting a teacher's website. I keep a list of these websites, along with passwords, in an e-mail inbox folder just in case kids "forget."

The reason that I and millions of other ADHDers have to go through these steps is that ADHD people have a positive self-illusory bias.[6] We truly believe we have mastered material and correctly recollected our homework and responsibilities without taking care to verify. ADHDers often feel ready for tomorrow's test, only to be dismally disappointed a week later when the test is given back. They casually leave school or work thinking they have everything they need.

When my students quickly dismiss my inquiries into homework and upcoming tests, I ask them, "How do I know that this is not your self-illusory bias coming out?" ADHDers must understand this falsely positive mindset or risk it consistently creating failure for them. In essence, becoming aware of this tendency creates a healthy dose of self-doubt.

With practice, this awareness can become automatic. When I leave my car, I automatically check to make sure I have my cell phone, keys, and wallet before I lock the car. When I leave a meeting, I always check to make sure that I have those same three items before exiting. When I leave a restaurant, I also search my seat and under the table to make sure nothing has fallen out.

This self-doubting mindset is one of the most powerful tools I use on myself and with my students and clients. The positive self-illusory bias is so ingrained that it can be quite difficult to break. But awareness of it has the potential to radically transform lives.

Tool #3: Be Playful

If you have managed to have a discussion with the ADHDer in your life about his or her goals, you have racked up a major accomplishment. More than likely you have gotten some pushback. Interactions with him or her are best when done in a playful manner. Seriousness activates our inner trip wires because we are so accustomed to being lectured to and criticized that we learn to instantaneously put up walls. Fun and playfulness, however, usually bypass our defenses and also help energize us.[7]

ADHD folks can often recall one teacher who was playful in class, perhaps even goofy. That's the class in which they excelled, and they end up remembering that teacher for the rest of their lives. Play is not just a frill or a bonus with ADHDers; it is a legitimate preference for interaction and communication.[8] Playfulness recharges an ADHDer's batteries.

It's easy to *tell* someone to be playful, but actually *being* playful can be difficult, especially for the serious-minded individual. Here are a few "games" that I regularly "play" with the ADHDers I see at Study Groups and those I coach over the phone:

- "The Director"—I use this game when a student or client is being negative, nasty, or annoying. I respond to the person as though I were a film director. To pull this one off, you have to get rid of sarcasm and find a place of genuine enjoyment within yourself, as if you were making a movie and the behavior you're seeing is exactly what the scene calls for. "Oh, that was masterful whining," I might say. "Can you heighten the nasal quality of your voice a bit?" Practice this tool with others or with yourself in the car before you actually try it out.

- "Funny voice"—ADHD individuals generally love funny accents and voices. When you cultivate this, you're playing with us, and that allows you to slip under our defenses. A message delivered with at least a little playful voice alteration has a greater likelihood of getting through. Again, you can practice these voices before you try them with the ADHDer in your life. Cecelia, mother of Michael, a fifteen-year-old ADHD boy who loved *The Simpsons*, used a handheld digital voice recorder to get snippets of the character Marge Simpson. She played them to herself over and over, and then recorded her attempts to make modifications. Whenever she gets irritated or is faced with noncompliance from her son, she pulls out Marge. Cecelia told me, "Marge gets through to Michael in ways that I cannot. She has almost eliminated the need for yelling in our household. I can hardly believe it!"

- "Pound it"—High-fives, gently pounding fists together, and elaborate handshakes give you a kinesthetic way to playfully connect with an ADHDer. It helps to engage in such gestures on a semiregular basis, as well as to come up with different variations. We don't like things to get stale.

- "Dance to the Music"—Kids at Study Groups will often use their iPhones to play rather loud music when they think I am out of earshot, and they also love to show each other You-Tube videos on my computers. Rather than burst in with my demand that the music be turned down, I often dance into the room and try to get into the beat. In this way, I am actually playing with them. They get the message in a positive and fun way, and they laugh at my pathetic dance moves!

Sometimes, video game breaks can get quite loud and raucous. Instead of yelling at them to keep it down, I try to come up with playful ways to get my point across. Here's one that has worked well: "You've done an admirable job of waking the dead; the trouble is, they want to go back to sleep now. Can you guys keep it down, please?"[9]

Being playful with an ADHDer has the potential to "dynamize" your communication. Look for ways to play!

Tool #4: Learning Centers

Many ADHD individuals, though not all, are poorly suited for sitting in one place for long periods of time. The stimulation of the environment around us gets old, and our brains are driven to find new stimulation. So we get distracted from whatever we're supposed to be doing. "Inattentive" ADHDers, on the other hand, prefer to stay in one place. They don't like having their endless daydreaming and flow of ideas interrupted. Interruption, however, can be an antidote for both types of ADHD individuals.

As with most of these strategies, I discovered this one purely by accident. Danny, a thirteen-year-old, came over one Sunday. He would work for about five minutes and then start goofing off or disrupting the people who were near him. I moved him several times. As a creative punishment, I had my assistant, Will, set the timer for five minutes. Each time it went off, Will was to randomly select a new place for Danny to work. Luckily my house, where I run the groups, is pretty big. So there were lots of places for him to go.

Will—who is affectionately called "The Guard"—loves to be creative and takes my orders quite literally. He had Danny work in the garage, on the back patio, and in just about every room in the house. When it was time for him to leave, I asked Danny if he had learned anything, hoping that he would be more mindful not to disrupt others in the future. He responded, "I learned that if I move around every five minutes, I get a lot of work done." I was flabbergasted. Danny had completed math assignments for the next three classes, in addition to finishing all his other homework, and he had managed to fill out a book report form that was a week overdue—and about which he had lied to the teacher, his parents, and me.

Danny continued this approach at Study Groups as well as at home, and I have used what I now call the "Learning Center Method" with more than a hundred students. I conference with kids who might find this useful when they first arrive, and we discuss where and for how long they will be working. Some have taken the approach one step further, placing books in different areas and leaving them there. So, they might work on math in the computer room and read *To Kill a Mockingbird* on one of the couches downstairs. They use a timer to determine when they move or simply work on a specific subject until they feel they have done what they can. "Learning Centers" can drastically increase productivity. I use it myself to get things done around the house.

Tool #5: The Cure for Writer's Block

I am part of an ADHD writers group. Seven of us meet once a month to compare notes, offer experience, and give advice. A few of us coach each other with weekly and sometimes daily calls. We have all noted that what succeeds in getting the writing process started today may not work tomorrow. We constantly develop new strategies. Many of the tools I use to help people with writing come from this group. It is yet another example of the power of mutual support.

For many ADHDers, creativity gets stunted the moment they sit down and try to put ideas on paper, so I engage my students in informal chats about their ideas. With some students, I take notes while we chat. I then transcribe my notes into a document on the computer. When students see their ideas recorded in this way, they are often jolted out of their lack of productivity. Taking notes doesn't work with some students. Once they realize what I am doing, they become inhibited. In these situations, I record the conversation using a small digital voice device (available at any Radio Shack). I put it in my shirt pocket, and they quickly forget they are being recorded. I then go to the computer and use a headset to listen to the conversation and transcribe their ideas.

With some students, I sit at the computer while they sit next to me. We talk back and forth to tease out ideas. Recently, I helped sixteen-year-old Brittany complete her term paper on the turmoil of the 1960s. She was so stressed about having to do a ten-page paper that she was almost completely blocked. My job centered on getting her to see that she understood her topic to a much larger extent than she realized.

> **Kevin:** So what is this paper about?
> **Brittany:** I don't really know.
> **Kevin:** Well, you already said that it has to do with the turmoil of the 1960s, right?
> **Brittany:** Yes.
> **Kevin:** You have to make a thesis statement about why those years are so important, right?
> **Brittany:** Yes.
> **Kevin:** Why were they important?
> **Brittany:** I have no idea!
> **Kevin:** What was different at the end of the 1960s?
> **Brittany:** Lots of things changed.
> **Kevin:** Like?
> **Brittany:** Lots of stuff.

Kevin: Just be specific. Did the world explode? Did World War III start?

Brittany: Women's rights, the war in Vietnam, race riots, protests, politics, television, and lots of other stuff.

Kevin: Were the changes that happened big changes or little changes?

Brittany: Big changes. They, like, totally changed the country.

Kevin: What's another word for totally?

Brittany: Basically?

Kevin: How about if you go to Google and look for a synonym and tell me which one you like?

Brittany: How about "fundamentally"?

Kevin: Sounds good to me. So now, make a thesis statement.

Brittany: This period of great turmoil fundamentally changed the nation.

Kevin: I think the statement might be a bit more powerful if you added something on the end of that to make it stronger.

Brittany: In lasting ways?

Kevin: What's the whole thesis then?

Brittany: This period of great turmoil fundamentally changed the nation in lasting ways?

Kevin: Does that feel good to you?

Brittany: It's better than I ever thought it was going to be.

Brittany seizes up with stress whenever she has to do a paper. I did nothing except talked her through it and convinced her, through our dialogue, that she understood her topic.

With some students, I have to be more explicit in pointing things out, but I always let them make their own thesis statement. My goal is to get them to see that they have a much better grasp of the material than they thought.

Self-doubt and criticism are the greatest barriers to effective writing. I build students' confidence by drawing out their ideas and then helping them structure what they put on paper. As for creativity in general, I recommend having a small notebook or, better yet, a cell phone to quickly save ideas that may come at any time. The best ideas often come when we're doing something else!

Lastly, I encourage students and clients to be mindful of whether they are in a creative or a critical mindset.[10] Most students mix these mindsets. They write the paper and make micro changes—spelling, grammar, punctuation, page setup—as they are brainstorming ideas. For most of us, this is poison. Criticizing our writing as we write usually shuts down the process. I learned this mindfulness technique from my comedy coach, Tony Vicich, who uses it to teach joke writing to his students. Being mindful of the difference between creating and criticizing can lead to productive explosions! I actually use two different computers to write: one for creating and one for criticizing what I have created.

Tool #6: Writing Templates

The Internet is full of useful tools to help structure your writing. To find some of these tools, simply search for your own variations of the following phrases: essay template, writing template, writing structure, essay structure. A particularly helpful site I often use has a "Thesis Builder" (see www.ozline.com/electraguide/). The site guides students by asking a series of simple questions. It then takes a student's answers and constructs a thesis. It is a great starting point for students who are stuck, and it gets them to see, in many cases, that they have great ideas but just need help structuring them.

When it comes to the classic "five-paragraph essay" format that most high school teachers assign, there are dozens of free templates available online that help students fill in the information needed to write an effective essay: thesis, topic sentences, supporting quotes, etc. Many sites offer tips for the nuts and bolts of the mechanics of writing: introducing and following up quotes, transitional phrases, and basic grammar. If structure is a problem, find structural support online. (See www.crls researchguide.org/NewOutlineMaker/NewOutlineMakerInput .aspx, www.experiment-resources.com/parts-of-a-research-paper .html, or http://dianahacker.com/pdfs/Hacker-Levi-MLA.pdf for examples.)

Tool #7: SparkNotes

Sparknotes.com offers summaries for virtually every book that middle and high school students read and for many at the college level too. In addition, and perhaps more importantly, SparkNotes has twenty-five-question quizzes to help students assess their knowledge of a particular book. These quizzes test readers on details found within the book and thus help determine whether a student has sufficient mastery before trying to grasp the deeper themes and motifs.

It is important to use this site as a supplement to reading, not a substitute. In my experience, kids who rely solely on SparkNotes and other such sites fare poorly on tests if they have not read the book.

Tool #8: Online Quizzes

"I know this stuff. I'm going to get an A." So goes the refrain parents frequently hear when they inquire whether their child is ready for a test. Many students who come to Study Groups struggle to accurately assess their level of mastery of material. Again, this positive self-illusory bias is often seen in ADHD kids. They truly believe they are headed for success and have absolutely no idea that, instead, they are headed straight for failure. "That test was going to be so easy," Matthew told me. "I thought I knew that stuff." The D- that he received was far from the A he was certain would be his. I hear this story continually. One of the greatest gifts Study Group participants learn is the ability to accurately assess their understanding of material.

"When you think you know the material," I tell students,

"study some more." I repeatedly remind students, "If you didn't do well on the last test, this time you have to do something different!" They have to learn not to trust their almost instinctual impulse to think they know the material; but more importantly, they must have some tools to ascertain their level of mastery.

With the growing importance of the Internet as a learning tool, textbook publishers now have supplementary study guides and resources to help students succeed. McDougal Littell, for example, has a website: www.classzone.com. The site gives students access to additional research and supplementary activities to enhance understanding, as well as review quizzes for each chapter of most of their textbooks. I make extensive use of these resources. I find online quizzes to be of the highest benefit. They not only help students assess their relative mastery of material, but they also give poor test-takers an opportunity to improve their skills. Most major textbook publishers have extensive online resources.

Tool #9: Teacher-Created Websites

In addition to the offerings of textbook publishers, many teachers write practice quizzes and study guides and make them available online. Chemistry teacher Mr. Guch, for example, has a website that he calls Cavalcade o' Chemistry.[11] He has worksheets and study guides from all his major chemistry topics, complete with detailed answer sheets. He makes it all available free of charge. Many of my students have used Guch's site to great advantage. One sophomore, David, went from a D in high school Chemistry class to an A, largely, I think, from using Guch's site. David had a teacher he found incredibly boring and he dreaded going to her class. He tuned out the whole time. Guch's website allowed an intelligent underachiever to learn the material at his own pace and use something he loved: the computer. He became a spark plug in the class. He began to answer the teacher's questions, and she noticed a huge difference in his behavior. He even caught a mistake she made. An excellent teacher, she praised David for being so observant in such circumstances, which completely turned him around with regard to chemistry. David is now majoring in biochemistry at the University of Michigan. ADHDers often have a lot of misdirected passion. Online resources can help that passion find a focus. Many useful sites can be found using a Google search. Again, I encourage a high level of Internet literacy. Google can be your best friend!

Tool #10: Edhelper.com

For a fifteen-dollar annual membership fee, Edhelper.com gives access to a variety of excellent study tools. Using the site's crossword puzzle generator, for example, I simply input clues from a particular unit that a student is working on and the site creates a great puzzle in about four seconds. The site has test and quiz generators for a variety of subjects, including math, grammar, vocabulary, social studies, and science. The material on the site is slanted toward younger children, but I have found it to be highly beneficial for middle and high school folks too.

Teachers at one local high school ask students to teach a lesson and prepare a subject-matter-appropriate activity. Maria, an eleventh grader, used the site to make crossword puzzles for her French class. The lesson she taught dealt with transportation vocabulary and the past tense of certain verbs. Although the assignment took all of ten minutes, it looked like she had put in hours. Edhelper.com is yet another example of how the Internet facilitates learning.

Tool #11: Make Up Practice Tests

Although online quizzes and tests are extremely useful, some students require more intense test-taking interventions. If a particular textbook offers only one practice quiz per chapter, that may not be enough. I have quite a few students whom I personally quiz, and I repeatedly go over material with them to ensure they are ready. It is not uncommon for me to be certain they are prepared and have them go on to perform poorly on the test. Such a test-taking issue often derives from anxiety, learning-style differences, poor working memory, poor retention, or simply the format of a test.

In such circumstances, I have found it most beneficial to make up my own test for the student. I only do this after I have obtained information from the teacher about testing format. I try to have my practice test mimic, to the closest degree possible, the test that a student will take. I familiarize myself with the way a particular teacher generally tests students and make my questions harder than those likely to be asked. I make up a test that looks similar to the one they will be taking.

I have many kids who struggle with high school biology. For Carol, a ninth grader who had trouble particularly with the multiple-choice format, I made up thirty questions, such as:

1. Which of the following is the correct RNA transcription of the following DNA sequence? A-C-T-A-T

   a. T-G-A-T-A
   b. G-A-C-G-T
   c. U-G-A-U-A
   d. G-U-A-G-U

I used the book and Carol's notes, as well as information provided to me by the teacher, to guide both questions and answer choices. When Carol finished the test, I gave her the answer sheet that I had already made up and had her correct her test. When she completed grading it, we talked about her thought process for each and every answer. She went into the actual test more conscious of how she was likely to make a mistake. After repeating this process for three chapters, Carol went from scoring in the fifties and sixties to averaging 83 percent on her biology tests for the remainder of the school year. I am certain that she has learned skills that will serve her for the rest of her life.

Max, a seventh-grade student with test-taking troubles, also struggled in science. He could not keep up with the sheer amount of terminology involved in Earth Science class. Since most of his tests were simply fill-in-the-blank, I just used his textbook to make up those types of questions. For one set of terms, I made two or three different tests that asked for the same terminology in different ways. This helped Max achieve greater mastery. Here are a few sample questions that I developed using his textbook:

1. When large blocks of the earth's crust drop down relative to other blocks, _____ mountains are formed.

2. Most of the world's major volcanic mountains are located at _____ boundaries.

3. When two tectonic plates push into one another, the place where they meet is called a _____   _____ .

As I always do with students, I had Max correct his tests and we talked about his responses and how his thought processes were responsible for the answers he chose. He realized the importance of *how* he thought about each question. This realization did not come from anything I explicitly told him, but rather grew naturally out of our discussions about the practice tests. His grades improved slowly, and by eighth grade, science had ceased being a huge problem for him.

For students like Carol and Max, practicing tests and discovering the way their minds work lead to success. I keep track of all the practice tests I make up so that I have them on hand the next time a student deals with the same subject matter. After eleven years, I have quite a collection.

Tool #12: A Wrong Can Make Things Right

Some students still have difficulty with test taking, even when they perform well on a practice test. Fifteen-year-old Ryan had struggled for years with disappointing test scores, causing him to develop a negative mindset. When he first came to see me, I was confident I could quickly help him turn things around, especially considering he had an IQ of 124. I pulled out every trick in the book, but test scores continued to languish in the sixties.

This young man became one of my pet projects. I knew in my gut that there had to be a way to help him. I met with his teachers and counselors, trying to get to the bottom of his issues. When I was close to giving up, I decided to try a new idea. He was studying sentences using the Spanish verb "gustar," which means "to be pleasing to." The way Spanish speakers say they like something is tricky, and most students have trouble mastering the structures. Ryan was no exception. The teacher had given him twenty sentences in Spanish using "gustar" constructions along with the English translations. I made up several different practice tests, none of which seemed to make any lasting difference, until I decided to use his negative mindset to his advantage. I made up a practice test in which he had to pick out the error. I used the teacher's sentences to make up three different quizzes. Some sentences had one error, some had two, and others were completely correct. He simply had to identify the error and make the correction. I had him take the quizzes repeatedly, alternating among different versions, and then I had him correct them himself. This technique seemed to make a difference, but I did not hold my breath.

He called me the next day, exuberant: "I think I passed this one!" We had to wait three days until the teacher put his score up on her website. Ryan got a B. He has continued to use this method with great success, and it has helped me discover his learning style. "I have to see what's wrong with something in order to remember it," he told me. "If I can see how a teacher might try to use information to trick me, then I will never forget it." The following are a few sentences of the first "negative" practice quiz I made for Ryan.

Pick out the error in the Spanish sentences below. Circle the error, and write the correction on the line below. If there is no error, write "correcto." Some sentences could have more than one error.

1. *The men like to work a lot also.*

   Los hombres les gusta trabajar también.

   (This should be "**A** los hombres.")

2. *The women do not like sports at all.*

   A las mujeres, no les gusta los deportes nada.

   (This should be "no les gusta**n**.")

3. *The girl does not like to play video games nor watch TV.*

   A la chica, no le gusta ni jugar videojuegos ni ver la tele.

   (Correcto)

I happen to speak Spanish, but that is not a requirement. I used sentences provided by the teacher to make sure they were similar to those that would be on the actual test. I try to call or e-mail teachers to tell them what I am up to. Most teachers are happy to send me information that I then use to create appropriate and useful practice quizzes.

Tool #13: Practice Tests Make Perfect

Passivity is the enemy of true learning. "It's too hard," Rory complained about his History of Religion class. "There are too many details to remember, and I can't keep them all straight." Rory felt at the mercy of what seemed, to him, to be the teacher's whims. He also had emotional blocks to studying religion because his agnostic parents had taught him that religion was ridiculous. Rory claimed, in addition, that the teacher tested the class on material they had not gone over. He was headed for failure. Rory felt powerless to do anything to change the situation.

In cases like this, I ask the students to become the teacher. I ask them to make up their own tests and think about how their teachers might manipulate the information to deceive them. This process requires them to be detectives. It teaches them to look out for information in their notes and in the textbook that would make good exam questions. "As you do tonight's reading assignment," I told Rory, "I want you to highlight anything that would make a good test question." After a few days, I sat down with him and we discussed ways of making the questions confusing and coming up with answer choices that might trick the students. I let him write the questions on his own, and when he had ten good questions, I asked him to get together with the teacher for feedback.

The teacher was thrilled with the young man's effort and talked to Rory as an equal, telling him what he liked about Rory's questions and how he might have done things differently. Rory felt empowered and realized through the interactions with the teacher that the man was not religious himself, but was simply teaching a body of information (I had called the teacher to prep him!). Here are a few of the questions Rory constructed:

1. Which of the following best describes the Catholic belief about non-Catholics being condemned by God?
   a. Only Catholics can get into heaven.
   b. Only Catholics and Christians can get into heaven.
   c. Catholics and only certain Christians can get into heaven.
   d. Those with a sincere heart can act according to God's law even if they are nonbelievers.

2. What word is used to describe the different Christian churches that have slightly different beliefs?

 a. Religious differentiations.
 b. Denominations.
 c. Grupus Christianius.
 d. Sects.

3. Who is a Cistercian monk who is considered one of the most influential spiritual writers of the twentieth century.

 a. Saint Thomas Aquinas.
 b. The Dalai Lama.
 c. Thich Nhat Hanh.
 d. Thomas Merton.

Rory found a way to organize his mind. "I am constantly on the lookout now," he told me, "for the kinds of things teachers test me on. Once I find something, I start thinking of ways teachers can play with it to make it confusing. When I do that, they can never trick me."

This technique can make an active learner out of an extremely passive one. I try to help students make a game out of it. If I can help them find a way to enjoy the process, all the better.

Tool #14: Discuss "OCD"

The "OCD" to which I refer is not obsessive-compulsive disorder. "OCD" in this case stands for a condition I have dubbed "over-complication disorder." It astonishes me how common this problem is. I became aware of it when I worked one summer with several teenagers on ACT test preparation. Bright kids, I noticed, sometimes scored poorly on the ACT. As I worked with a few in particular, I discussed their wrong answers with them. I was amazed at how often they would say things like, "Oh, I was going to pick that one." As I probed their thought processes, I realized, to my amazement, that many of the students were more likely to get easy problems wrong than hard ones. It seemed as though they did not trust their instincts on easy questions and unconsciously made the questions more difficult. Above-average students with ADHD and/or anxiety issues often display "OCD." Practice tests and quizzes do help, but "OCD" kids also need extensive discussion to make them conscious of how they behave and think, thus making change possible. I have seen students struggle for years before finally figuring it out. It is important to engage them in an ongoing dialogue, because they can get frustrated and feel that the situation will never change.

When students consistently demonstrate that they knew the right answer and fret over the fact that they chose the wrong one, "OCD" is probably at work. They will chastise themselves by saying, "How could I have been so stupid?" They ask, "What was I thinking?"

Fifteen-year-old Jenny performed brilliantly on practice tests and wowed me with her mastery of material. Yet, in two classes during her sophomore year, U.S. History and Biology, she could not score above a 70 percent. I e-mailed both of her teachers apprising them of the extensive measures we were taking to help Jenny succeed. Both of them were shocked and had assumed that Jenny was simply not studying enough (it is important to keep teachers informed). We arranged a meeting and came up with a plan. Jenny was to meet with each of them on the morning of the test and then arrange to meet with them to go over test results after they had been graded. In addition, both teachers agreed to check in with Jenny during tests to see if her "OCD" was in check. It took more than two months, but Jenny eventually broke through and started getting the As that she deserved. In her words, "'OCD' still operates in my head, but now I recognize it for what it is and it no longer controls me."

I have found it helpful simply to tell kids that they have "OCD." Putting a name to an unconscious enemy that has dogged their academic careers instantly gives them a measure of power over it. I stroke their egos by telling them, "Smart people make stupid mistakes."

Smart or Stupid: Reading Ahead

In my early years, I was always hearing how "smart" I was. I regularly overheard my sisters, my mother, and scores of family friends say, "Did you hear Kevin's new word of the day? You're not going to believe what he just said." I felt special, and even though I struggled a lot in school, that inner sense of intelligence never left me. It's been one of the most important contributing factors in my eventual success.

My teachers told me a different story, however. In second grade, after starting out in a high-level reading group, I was moved into a lower reading group. I had been tested at several years above that grade level, so I knew I could read. And I knew I was "smart." OK, so it may have had something to do with not doing the work, or goofing around, or pulling a girl's pigtails one day, but that's beside the point.

After some punishment time in the corner, I was eventually moved to the lower reading group with the promise of being allowed back into the "smart" group with good behavior. One day, while reading together in the "dumb" group, I found myself enjoying the book and flying twenty pages ahead of everyone else on my own. When called upon, I had no idea what I was supposed to read, I stumbled, and I was kept in the lower reading group for the rest of the year. That I remember this now, more than thirty years later, testifies to the impact it had on me. I began to wonder if I was stupid, but the even more destructive message was that little would be expected of me if I acted dumb.

So many ADHDers approach school, careers, and life believing they are stupid or that it's useless to try to prove otherwise. To have any chance at success, we must first chip away at this destructive delusion.

Tool #15: Confront the Procrastinator

We ADHD folks are among the world's greatest procrastinators. We leave barely enough time to complete an assignment or study the material, and we often push the envelope so far that we do not even have enough time. Parents of ADHDers fight this battle, usually unsuccessfully, for years. "I can't understand why you just don't start sooner!" they will say. Parents generally are not aware of the neurological reasons for this seemingly illogical behavior.

The ADHD brain has lower overall activity in a few key cerebral regions. We need the intensity and stress of the "last minute" to get the brain functioning more effectively so we have enough drive and attention to complete a task. Some of us thrive under this pressure, while others become overwhelmed. With both types of individuals, there is a high price to be paid.

One sixteen-year-old student, David, countered my arguments against procrastination by saying, "If I get the paper done, what does it matter how I do it?" Staying up late to cram or complete a paper causes a sleep deficit that strains the individual for at least a few days afterward. Family members see an irritable and ill-tempered person who is hard to be around. ADHD folks often require more sleep than the average person, so a sleep deficit can cause more serious disruptions in the person's life. Cramming for a test doesn't usually lead to the best grades. Writing a paper at the last minute eliminates the potential for editing and improvement. "Your procrastination throws your whole life out of balance," I told David, "and prevents you from doing your best work." David, like many ADHDers, had grown so accustomed to chaos in his life that he was very resistant to letting it go. Chaos and drama light up the brain, and unless an ADHD person can find a different way to "turn on," giving up procrastination will be very difficult.

The tendency of ADHDers to delay starting a task derives from biological forces. The first step in dealing with the situation is to help the individual recognize the behavior, understand its cerebral underpinnings, and then identify its destructive effects. The only way I know to break dependence on procrastination is to help the individual find other ways of creating intensity. Many of the tools in this book are devoted to this pursuit.

> *Sleep is a serious problem for ADHDers. More than half of ADHD children have difficulty with falling asleep as well as feeling tired when awakening, and roughly 40 percent have issues with waking up in the middle of the night.[12] Research suggests that ADHD is not the direct culprit in sleep problems, pointing instead to the multiple comorbid conditions often accompanying ADHD.[13] My anxiety, for example, seems to kick in as soon as my head hits the pillow, a finding also reported by many of my students and clients. I stop drinking coffee at 5 p.m., limit computer and video game stimulation after 10 p.m., and try to perform light and gentle stretches right before bed. I also find the white noise of a fan to be particularly helpful in calming my mind. Sleep problems can exacerbate many of the symptoms of ADHD, and so should be dealt with swiftly!*

Tool #16: Audio Books and Movies

Many ADHD young people struggle with reading, especially with books that do not intrinsically interest them. For quite a few students, this means every book they are assigned in school. Even if they read the book, their minds wander. The perfunctory nature of how they sit down to read ensures that they remember very little afterward. Audio books are valuable tools that help ignite the mind so that students retain more of what they read. Using two senses, vision and hearing, instead of one often makes a world of difference.

Many young people cheat, however, by only listening to the book and not following along visually. This is a huge mistake because it eliminates the opportunity for improving one's reading.

Students should *always* follow along in the book. If a student has done this and then wants to review by listening only, that is fine.

Local libraries have audio versions of most major works, and if they do not, they can almost always borrow one from another library. Interlibrary loans take time, so make sure the student is communicating with the teacher about upcoming books so they can be procured in time. Also, availability can be limited due to many students in your area reading the same book at the same time. Amazon.com is an inexpensive remedy for this situation. The site has just about everything, often at a low price.

Movies are no substitute for reading the book, but they can, in certain situations, be incredibly helpful. I had two fourteen-year-old boys, Brian and Tony, in a Study Group. They happened to be in the same ninth-grade English class. Both boys complained profusely about their English teacher. They also despised each and every book they had been forced to read in ninth grade. I decided on an experiment to see whether I could pull off the impossible: getting two hyperactive fourteen-year-old ADHDers interested in Shakespeare.

Both boys bemoaned their upcoming assignment of reading the prologue to *Romeo and Juliet*. My attempts at trying to make the story relevant to their lives fell on deaf ears. Tony told me, "You're using the same lines our English teacher did." Obviously, I needed a new strategy.

I went to the library and looked through the different versions of *Romeo and Juliet* that were available on DVD. I came across the 1996 modern-day version with Leonardo DiCaprio. Begrudgingly, they agreed to watch. By the scene early in the movie, featuring the altercation between the Capulets and Montagues, they were hooked. Both boys went on to do well on the tests and participate in class discussions. "Ryan," his teacher said, "why haven't you been like this the whole year?" Getting high marks on all the work associated with *Romeo and Juliet* was the only thing that allowed him to pass the class and not have to take summer school.

Most video versions of Shakespeare are not as engaging as the one we used, but still, libraries have all of Shakespeare's plays on video. It is important to make sure that students do not substitute a video for reading, but for visual learners, a movie can really help.

Tool #17: Read, Listen, and Exercise!

Audio books are effective, I think, largely because they allow a person to process using two different senses and thus get more of the brain involved in the task. If we add aerobic activity to the mix, we take that processing ability even further. Much scientific evidence confirms that the ADHD brain functions more effectively after, as well as during, aerobic activity. I don't need scientists to tell me this. My mother had me using this strategy in ninth grade when I hit the academic wall. "Why don't you make cassette tapes of the material," my mother suggested, "and then listen to them while you ride your bike." My retention went way up, and the amount of time I needed to master material went way down. I had found the magnitude of material in school overwhelming at the beginning of ninth grade. Using this simple technique, I had no more problems managing the homework load. I used it to study all through high school and college.

For students with serious retention issues, I recommend that they study on a treadmill or other exercise device. This needs to be done with safety in mind, however. If the person is physically awkward or clumsy, this technique should be practiced with someone else in the room. I had one student get seriously injured while reading on a treadmill. If there is any chance of getting hurt, we ADHDers are good at finding it. Be careful!

Together, the students and I make tapes or CDs of their academic material that they can listen to while exercising. If they listen, follow along in the book, and exercise, they are using multiple senses to help retain information. "It's like my brain actually starts working when I'm on the treadmill," twelve-year-old Matt said. "It's the only time I feel like I get anything done." Matt struggled in eighth grade with Shakespeare's *Julius Caesar*. It was an incomprehensible jumble until he listened and read while on the exercise machine. "Why can't I be like this all the time?" he asked me. My hope is that with continued application of these methods, Matt's retention will increase. For now, he's found something that works and allows him to succeed in English, a class in which he has always teetered on failure.

Many students study while exercising, while others work out before studying. Studying paired with exercise is a winning combination. Exercise can be employed along with most other strategies in this book. Claire, a high-energy eight-year-old ADHDer, became a times tables whiz once we practiced them together on a trampoline! Again, this sort of thing has to be done with great caution. I advise supervision and that every possible safety precaution be taken.

When a student experiences writer's block, I often have him or her get on the treadmill. A few minutes later, I stop by, we discuss the paper or project, and solutions to the block usually emerge. With David, a hyperactive fifteen-year-old with an incredibly short attention span, I made flash cards and the two of us would go out for a jog. I asked him questions on the run. Exercise. Exercise. Exercise.

Tool #18: With a Little Help from My Friends

Between middle and high school, most teens begin to rely less on their parents for support and more on their peers. This developmental step has interpersonal as well as significant academic implications. ADHD folks often have difficulty making and keeping friends, so as they move to the college years, a time when reliance on peers is crucial, they can be at a distinct disadvantage.[14] My ADHD Study Groups help fill in the gap by teaching social skills in a point-of-performance social situation. Young people work on school assignments and develop social contacts at the same time. I realize the risk of young people becoming dependent on me and the groups, so I encourage them to study with friends at the library, a coffee shop, or someone's house. Although parents worry that such study outings are not productive, such outings are an important part of emotional growth.

We ADHDers must work on our social skills because support from peers can be a deciding factor in whether we succeed in life. Therapy and coaching can help us monitor ourselves so that we do not monopolize conversations or frequently interrupt others. For me, an ongoing internal dialogue helped me to accomplish this. I remember in high school literally telling myself things like "Shut up or you're going to turn these people off." I did succeed in making and keeping a few friends. In Advanced Placement European History, a few friends and I got together weekly to split up the fifty terms we had to define. Doing all fifty by myself took hours, but by working with friends, it only took about an hour. I had people I could call in case I had forgotten homework, which was often an issue. There was an academic camaraderie; we would talk about upcoming tests and papers and what our plans were for doing the work. These conversations helped keep me focused and stimulated. Improving social skills leads to better peer relationships, which exert a subsequent impact on school performance.

I find that simply sharing experiences with other ADHDers can greatly improve social skills. Frank and honest discussions with peers who have endured similar struggles pack a positive punch. At our local CHADD chapter, coordinator and psychologist Fran Parker puts on a yearly teen panel during which teens talk about their difficulties and successes. This year we had more than forty attendees. Such events lessen the stigma of being ADHD and provide much-needed optimism that success will happen. It is much easier to take advice from a fellow ADHDer.

Find opportunities to socialize with other ADHD people, and work with therapists, coaches, and mentors on advancing social skills. If you're a parent, find other parents and make play dates, set up game nights, and have kids play video games together instead of alone. If your adult loved one has ADHD, try to get him or her to join CHADD, take the Dale Carnegie course to help build social skills, or get involved at a local church. Volunteering with religious organizations and nonprofits is a great way to meet people. Implement the lessons in this book and get creative in helping your ADHD loved one expand his or her social network.

Tool #19: The Timer

Many people who come to Study Groups lose track of time. Some get lost in their own thoughts while others socialize, play games on their laptops, and otherwise fool around. I use timers with some kids to make completing an assignment a more intense experience. "If you get your science questions done in twenty-five minutes," I told a student, "then you can have a twenty-minute video game break." Kids not only want to have that break because they love the game, but more importantly, it allows them to hang out with other kids and have fun. I am very careful to create a time frame that I believe is attainable. I do not want to set up a student for failure!

When dealing with ADHD, we often have to trick the mind into snapping to attention. Creating intensity is a great way to do that. I might say, "I am giving you twenty minutes to get your math assignment done. If you do not get it done in that time, you're going to have to keep coming back to it."

ADHD folks struggle with time management as well. The timer helps make them more aware of their productivity or lack thereof. By using timers with students over the course of two to three months, I have seen productivity rise significantly, along with an increased ability to manage time.

Tool #20: Get a Little Crazy

When it comes to ADHDers absorbing information—and then successfully regurgitating it for tests or presentations—creativity is the most potent ally. A variety of methods should be employed to see which ones produce the best results. Some people learn best with visual or auditory cues, while hands-on learners take in information most effectively in a kinesthetic, or physically involved, manner. These folks are the pencil tappers and leg shakers who drive teachers crazy. Auditory and visual learners find the academic world much more in line with their learning styles than we kinesthetic learners do.

I find with ADHDers that a combination of approaches works well. For that reason, I urge you to employ as many of the tools in this chapter as possible and use them as guides to come up with your own strategies.

I am definitely a hands-on learner. I, like many ADHDers, learn best by doing and am receptive to information when I am in motion. When I am preparing for a workshop or lecture, I make large mind maps and post them on the walls. I make study recordings with my digital handheld voice recorder, and then I listen to them in the car, gym, or on a walk. If there are points that strike me as particularly important, I associate them with different textures, adding a multisensory element to my preparation. It may sound crazy to the outsider, but when I struggle to remember information, I bury my hand in a bowl of sand and move it around while I am studying. In this way, the feel of the sand becomes linked with the data I need to absorb, making it much easier to recall. I also use incense and scented candles when I am reading to make the activity more stimulating and memorable. The more senses I involve in my learning, the more likely I will be able to quickly and correctly recollect the information.

When my writing progress slows, I often take a brisk walk or do abdominal crunches. I have an electric abdominal belt that sometimes does the trick too. Writer's block is incredibly frustrating, but I see frustration as opportunity. I use a stress ball to physically express my frustration, and this simple act is often sufficient to get me back to productivity. When I am really in a pinch and ideas totally stop flowing, I will take my laptop into unusual places. I have worked in the dark in my closet, in the garage, and at the café at the Detroit Institute of Arts. I even rented a hotel room for the night. That turned out to be a bad idea, because I don't have cable TV at home, and it was just too much of a temptation. My friend Barb's cabin up north has been a great blessing for my writing because there is neither Internet nor cell phone coverage. I have been most productive up there.

You have to get a little crazy. The more unusual and unorthodox your ideas, the greater the likelihood they will work. When you find strategies that lead to success, don't get stuck on them, however. Stay open to new ideas. Let flexibility, creativity, and diversity be your guides.

CREATE INTENSITY

I have a friend whom we'll call Joe. In contrast to me, he loves routines. A health fanatic and vegetarian, he eats almost the same thing at the same time every day and has a walking regimen that follows the same exact path. His favorite show is *Monk*. Regularity and predictability comfort him. "I feel safe and secure in my routines," he told me. One of the reasons that Joe and I have remained great friends for the past twenty years is that we are exact opposites in the way we approach life . . . and the fact that he's walked by my house every day for sixteen years. We complement each other. He has given me a steady flow of practical advice in matters ranging from finances to relationships. He has helped me create stability during stressful times. I asked him recently if he had thought about why we had stayed friends these many years. "You're fun to be around," he answered. "You're spontaneous and wacky, which are two things that I desperately need in my life . . . over and over on a regular and predictable basis." Joe helps me find structure and I help him lighten up.

Joe's brain is designed for routine. He moved to Arizona four years ago, and after just two weeks in his new house, he had established his walking circuit, compared prices and quality to settle on the market where he bought his fruit and vegetables, and arranged his apartment to look identical to his previous one. He is now on a mission to get me to move to Arizona so he can walk by my house every day. Joe felt anxious without his routines when he moved and could not wait to reestablish them. My brain, and those of most ADHDers, struggles to maintain routines. When something becomes rote and predictable, the activity level in our brains actually goes down. This is scientifically measurable.

ADHDers often perform phenomenally when a new semester of school or a new job starts, but after a few weeks or months, the novelty wears off. Parents will delight in their child's solid performance early in the semester and many hold out hope that a new page has been turned. Their hopes deflate when they realize that high grades were a temporary blip on the radar. Old patterns return, and they berate themselves and their child. "Here we go again," one mother told me after she had discovered that the As her son had achieved in the first month of school were mostly Cs and Ds by November due to missing assignments. "I thought he had actually changed."

THE DIP

I tell parents and young people to expect what I call The Dip. I give this same advice to adult clients who run into difficulties with their jobs. The newness will fade, and consequently the ADHD brain will stop functioning optimally. This situation must be expected as part of the normal course of events. One way out of The Dip is to find imaginative ways to create intensity.

I owe my success in high school largely to the intensity that the environment provided, as well as to a desire to avoid a beating. It got my brain started and showed me that I could attain the grades I always felt I deserved. The experience of those four years taught me that the sky was the limit. No matter what happened, I knew from that point that I could do anything I wanted, provided I could find the right mix of tools.

TOO MUCH INTENSITY?

Creating intensity is the best method I know to help an ADHDer. But those who spend a lot of time around us ADHDers frequently complain that we are too intense. When they say this, we just stare at them. "Chris vibrates on a different frequency," Sandy told me about her sixteen-year-old son. "My brain frequently feels fried when I am around him." Although Sandy had spent countless hours helping her son keep up with his schoolwork, by his junior year, she was ready to give up.

ADHD individuals' loved ones must find a way to stay connected and not give up hope. Supporting one of us through school or a career requires the same endurance as a marathon runner has. While we ADHDers need to find ways to make routines more exciting and engaging, those close to us need to figure out a way to not let us get under their skin. Supporting an ADHDer can feel like a roller-coaster ride of incredible highs and unforeseen lows that seem to come from nowhere. Our propensity for snatching defeat from the jaws of victory tries the patience of even our most steadfast supporters.

It is useful to understand how the ADHD brain works and what kinds of difficulties you can expect when trying to create change or assisting an ADHDer in that process. I recommend arming yourself with knowledge and a whole lot of tools!

WHAT IF NOTHING WORKS?

If you try a variety of methods and nothing seems to work, then it may be time to consider a neuropsychological evaluation. A significant number of ADHD folks suffer from coexisting learning disabilities and challenges. Martin, a fifteen-year-old ADHDer, had struggled for years in school but had managed to eke out passing grades through a combination of a charming personality and a commitment to doing all the homework. In high school, as grades became more heavily dependent on tests, he really started to get into trouble. I rolled out every trick I knew on this hardworking young man, and our work together yielded a very modest benefit: an average increase of 7 percentage points on tests overall. After five months of disappointing results, his mother had Martin tested by a neuropsychologist who found an expressive and receptive language processing issue. The bottom line is that he had difficulty understanding and expressing spoken and written language. This finding led to appropriate accommodations in school, as well as twice-weekly sessions with a speech pathologist. In addition, the young man received accommodations on the ACT test. With all the strategies and assistance now in place, Martin's grades have improved, and he feels a lot more confident about prospects for his future. When dealing with ADHD, consider that other learning disabilities and challenges may be involved.

ADHD is a complex condition, and no single approach works for every ADHDer. As you work with yourself or a loved one with ADHD, you are ultimately helping to unravel a mystery and find missing pieces to a puzzle. You are on a journey of discovery that will help you better understand yourself, other people, and the world around you. It is easy and understandable to become pessimistic. I have seen so many amazing success stories that I am an optimist and have come to see ADHD as representing a set of opportunities.

COMIC RELIEF

Lest you get too serious about ADHD, I end this chapter with a few jokes. The worst thing that can happen when you're dealing with an ADHDer is to lose your sense of humor!

- Two ADHDers walked into a bar. They forgot why they were there.

- If you play video games, while watching TV, while talking on the phone, while you eat a day-old piece of pizza you found under the couch, you might be ADHD.

- If you ever find yourself running circles around your couch, yelling, "Woo, woo, woo, woo!" followed by, "This is fun," you might be ADHD.

- If everything in your house has been broken three times—once when your kid was five, once when he was ten, and once when he was fifteen—he might be ADHD.

- If, when you ask your kid, "How many times do I have to tell you," she answers, "Forty-five," she might be ADHD . . . and a smart aleck. And, by the way, she is actually correct.

- If you pull up to your local junkyard to buy a car part and the manager says, "Don't bring your kid in; he'll break stuff," your kid might have ADHD.

- If your kid's clothes are all over the floor and his closet is full of everything except clothes, he might have ADHD.

CHAPTER 7

OVERCOMING THE ODDS

*"Success is to be measured not so much by the position
that one has reached in life as by the obstacles . . .
overcome while trying to succeed."*
Booker T. Washington

Mounds of research support the view that ADHD can lead to severe and life-altering impairment. Intellectual development, academic performance, and adaptive functioning all suffer because of ADHD. ADHD also correlates to a significantly higher risk for learning disabilities, motivational difficulties, and sleep problems. Because many ADHDers have a lower appreciation for future consequences, some research suggests a "reduced concern for health-conscious behavior, such as exercise, proper diet, and moderation in using legal substances."[1] Some theorists have even suggested reduced life expectancy for ADHDers. The developmental drawbacks of ADHD can seem almost overwhelming, especially for those who suffer not just from the associated inattention and impulsivity but from some of the troubling comorbidities as well. ADHD definitely does make life more complicated.

In spite of the odds, I witness success stories every day. I am blessed with brave individuals who not only buoy me with their determination but also affirm me in the path I have chosen.

When I get writer's block, sometimes just thinking of the successes of my students and clients is enough to jolt me out of it. Brian, a former student who is now twenty-nine years old, had not only ADHD but also dyslexia. He needed an extra year to get through law school and took the bar exam five times before he passed. But he is now a lawyer who works as an assistant prosecutor. "Success, for me," Brian said, "has been an exercise in compensating for my instinctual impulses. So often, one step forward was followed by two steps back. School was just not set up for people like me."

For many, school can be an incubator for success. For ADHDers, it is often a breeding ground for failure. Institutions that stress routine, mundane rhythms, organization, follow-through, and planning will rarely value an ADHDer. When told how to surmount an obstacle, the ADHD mind instantly busies itself scheming ways to go around, under, or through it. "He spends so much energy fighting the system," one father told me. "If he spent half as much doing things the *right* way, he would be overwhelmingly successful."

The snag is that we actually like doing things our own way. Although this may seem troubling, examples abound of ADHDers finding innovative and unorthodox methods to achieve success. New ideas and shortcuts energize us. Many of us are natural innovators and entrepreneurs. We instinctually think out of the box. If we get proper support, receive positive messages, and attain some self-understanding, these traits are exceptional assets.

FROM SLACKER TO ACADEMIC STAR

Your old grandmother says,
"Maybe you shouldn't go to school. You look a little pale."
Run when you hear that.
A father's stern slaps are better.
Pray for a tough instructor
to hear and act and stay within you.
—Rumi, Sufi mystic and poet

When I speak about my elementary and middle school years, people are curious about how I managed to make the shift to being an A-student in high school. Like Michael Corleone in *The Godfather*, I had longed to make the jump in my educational "business" from trickery to legitimacy. The lying was getting old—and had stopped working—so I was desperate for an opportunity to prove myself. I was moving into manhood and noticed a need to make my mark and, to paraphrase the immortal words of Marlon Brando in *On the Waterfront*, "to be somebody." I was too small and not talented enough to play sports at my high school. Family members, friends, teachers, and even random strangers had talked about how smart I was, so I thought I could do well in school and make my mark in academics.

Having relied on deception for the previous eight years, I didn't know how to bring about the transformation I longed for. ADHDers often experience this. Deception and trickery are so often successfully employed by us ADHDers that by the time we hit our academic wall—meaning our tricks no longer work— we are developmentally behind, which makes academic failure a vicious cycle to break.

Although desperation to get revenge on Mulch, my eighth-grade teacher, propelled me to change, I had other great allies at my new school: my teachers. I was blessed in ninth grade with four teachers who scared the living crap out of me. Three of them were members of an order of priests that ran the school. They were tough. Those of us who had to endure their toughness did not even think of complaining to our parents. That would have been a fruitless endeavor. These were holy men, and at that time, parents still thought priests could do no wrong. My friend Matt's father had no sympathy when Matt recounted being thrown to the floor during math class: "So, you got beat up today, son. Father Baumeister taught you a good lesson, didn't he?" Joe's father, like almost all Catholic parents at that time, always assumed the student to be in the wrong: "You got hit? You probably deserved it!"

Some of these men, such as Father Baumeister, had incredible gifts for teaching. Father Donoher, however, stands out among them all. He made up memorable songs to teach about the Bible, Catholic theology, and ancient history. His greatest work, *The Bible Beat,* contains twenty verses that cover Jewish history from Abraham to the Maccabean Revolt. My favorite verse is about Alexander the Great:

> Now "Al" who really loved the bottle
> Had been taught by Aristotle
> So he also loved his Greek
> Thought it was the way to speak
> Made Greek Culture all the rage (uh, huh, huh)
> And ushered in the Hellenistic Age

The man was a mastermind who made learning fun. He did impressions, performed shuffle dances, and told interesting story after interesting story. He was a genius, a showman, a teacher, and a stand-up comedian all rolled into one. Largely due to his class, school for me went from being a mundane and grating obligation to an entertaining and infinitely stimulating experience. As soon as I walked into Father Donoher's classroom, I relaxed into my true self. I felt that it was OK to be me.

Father Kowalski was my homeroom counselor and French teacher. He was also inspiring, but in a very different way. He took teaching very seriously and thought meticulously about his methods. "Language is a skill that must be practiced," he told me in ninth grade. "You learn language by speaking more than you do by studying a book." He drilled us every day using songs and movement. Not doing homework had physical consequences. If you didn't do your homework or you spoke even a word of English in his class, you were likely required to do ten, maybe as many as fifty, push-ups. What a great situation for an ADHDer! He neither shamed nor belittled us, however. He simply set up repercussions that were dispassionately, if not gently, administered. I give Father Kowalski great credit for recognizing and nurturing my ability to acquire foreign languages. He inspired me to reach for mastery.

Early in my first semester of ninth grade, the school held an assembly for academic mastery for those who won the Gabriel Richard Award, an honor that required a 3.6 grade point average and no grade below a B. For some reason, my English teacher, Mr. DuBois, singled me out later that day and told me he thought I should strive to get that award. It was such a shocking assertion that I did not immediately dismiss it, even though it seemed far-fetched. He believed in me, something no other teacher had ever done. He checked in with me often to see if I was on track, offering plenty of suggestions along the way. As I consider the whole matter now, I can feel the buzz that beat inside me after Mr. DuBois issued his inspiring challenge. Because of Mr. DuBois's faith in me and his support, I received the Gabriel Richard Award every semester of high school.

Mr. DuBois's class was perfect for an ADHDer. He built in lots of humor and sometimes allowed the class to teeter on the brink of chaos. Just when things seemed to be getting a little out of control, his zany control-freak side would kick in. He maintained a class rhythm that was structured, but unpredictable—perfect for someone like me. I had always loathed English class, but he made me love to read and write. He made literature come alive, and he made diagramming sentences a game. Mr. DuBois was yet another great blessing I received during that transformative first year of high school.

Another source of inspiration was punishment, which was meted out in creative ways. A JUG, or "Judgment Under God," was the equivalent of a detention, except that JUGs involved raking leaves, washing walls, cleaning toilets, and other relatively unpleasant activities. As explained to me by the school's dean, "When you break your commitments to the school, you are out of integrity. Service to the community is one of the best ways to get back into integrity." The theoretical framework for JUGs aside, this system helped me go from being serially tardy to always being on time to school and my individual classes. This was a major step forward in my development. The application of intense and unpredictable stimuli did much to set me on the right track.

The normal and mundane rhythms of academic life are not usually sufficient to arouse the ADHD brain. Danger, discomfort, and intensity, however, can really get our ADHD brains active. Many of us require extreme forms of stimulation to allow us to perform tasks and concentrate. The silver lining is that we can often blossom under pressure. Thom Hartmann has talked much about the hunter archetype as a way of viewing ADHD.[2] According to Hartmann's persuasive thesis, hunters are those individuals who respond quickly, sometimes instantaneously, to new stimuli. They thrive on the excitement of the chase and can switch gears at a moment's notice. These are exactly the same attributes that get ADHD kids in trouble when we put them into the classroom and expect them to sit at a desk all day, while bombarding them with information that interests them very little. Ah, but add an element of danger and excitement, and the ADHD brain begins to activate.

THE BEAT OF A DIFFERENT DRUM

Although I did well in college, I grew increasingly bored with academics. I began to procrastinate more and suffered from the same sort of boredom that plagued me in my first eight years of school. I took several semesters off to indulge other "interesting" pursuits. I went into a power-washing business with a friend. I sold contract after contract, but he insisted we hire employees to do all the work. All our money went into labor costs, and I had to work three jobs to pay back my mother the $3,500 she had lent us to start up the business. My "friend" paid back none of the money. This was my first lesson in my tendency to associate with the wrong sorts of people. Not having learned my lesson, I went on to start three other unsuccessful business ventures with this same individual. Sometimes I learn at incredibly slow speeds, but I still have fun trying something new.

I drove a moving van cross-country for five months. It turned out that the owner had illegally leased the vehicles we were using; they were not supposed to go out of state. A routine traffic stop alerted police to the situation. I was almost arrested in Santa Rosa, New Mexico, for my boss's misdeeds. I "escaped" on a Greyhound bus in the middle of the night. I had no interest in sorting out the owner's web of lies with the police. I later learned that the threat of arrest was merely a police ploy to find out what I knew; I had done nothing wrong.

During this period of exploration, I talked my way into several jobs that went completely against my grain. I was the cleaning supervisor for the food concessions at a horse racing track outside of Detroit. I eventually left that job because it bored me to death. Talking my way into such a detail-oriented position is an example of my persuasive powers.

More attuned to my skill set, I sold Irish imports at Irish festivals all over the country. My mother and I were in business together. She had the idea, and the two of us worked tirelessly to make it a success. We drove up and down the East Coast every summer, while also making the rounds to Chicago, Minneapolis, and Milwaukee. We went to so many Irish events that there are certain Irish folk tunes I can no longer bear. This venture was perfect for ADHDers: two days of intensity, followed by four days of rest and then a day of travel to a new location. I became Kevin "O'Casey" from County Leitrim, Ireland, at these events, speaking with an Irish brogue. I picked County Leitrim because my Irish-born friend, Joe Gaynor, told me, "Nobody over here is from Leitrim. They'll never catch you." I did get caught, however, when a Leitrim-born man demanded to know what town I was from! Appreciative of my little ruse, he sat with me to help elaborate on my story so that I would not get caught the next time. (We decided that I was from Carrick-on-Shannon.) I love the Irish! I had great fun, and this business venture pretty much paid for college, although it necessitated taking off several semesters. My mother was also able to take several trips to Europe with her church choir, fulfilling a lifelong dream.

While these activities represent only a few of my extracurricular forays, they serve to show how boredom sent me into adventure. I am a hands-on learner, whom theories without practical application do not engage.

For this reason, finding a graduate program was incredibly difficult. Given my interest in ADHD, psychology and social work seemed appropriate. But I ultimately decided that I did not want to sit in an office doing therapy, nor did pure research hold any appeal. After several starts and stops, I determined that I was probably not going to get a graduate degree. Luckily, I found a progressive educational institution offering the ability to individualize a master's program. I decided to study ADHD and was able to choose a mentor with whom I had already worked. For instructors I chose were experts from universities all over the country who had specialties in areas that were important for my work. I covered ADHD diagnosis, treatment, learning styles, and neurobiology, and I was able to build in practicum experiences with hospitals and clinics. I was completely engaged in the degree and loved every minute of it. I tell this story because it highlights the fact that there are resources available that allow us to get degrees in nontraditional ways. We can follow many different paths. The book *Colleges That Change Lives* is a great resource for finding these sorts of programs. The author also has a website: www.ctcl.org. Unfortunately, too many of us suffer trying to fit in, rather than seek unique approaches to complement our innate skills and gifts.

WILD BRILLIANCE

Steve's story demonstrates the tremendous suffering some ADHDers endure before finally finding a workable path. Boredom, mischief, and borderline antisocial behavior characterized Steve's school years. The high-energy and risk-taking nine-year-old skipped the bus in favor of "shagging." This activity, in which I also engaged as a young man, involves nothing sexual, but rather squatting on snow-packed streets and grabbing hold of the bumper of passing cars to hitch a fun-filled and adrenaline-packed ride, punctuated by the twin threats of being caught by the police or being hurled under the moving vehicle. Steve easily recounts extracurricular antics such as "shagging," but he strains to recall the grim details of his time in school. "There was one incident," Steve said, "when I was forced to stay in a coat closet in my teacher's room for the entire day. I still cannot remember what I had done, but I distinctly recall the prison-cell-like quality of the closet. I felt like a criminal. That still sticks with me." Steve suspects that there are more memories like this waiting to be uncovered.

Whether he was at school or in his parents' home, Steve longed to be outside. "I wanted to be free," he said. "It was like my parents and teachers were trying to imprison me or put me in a straitjacket. Being outside and in nature made me feel alive and unfettered." Steve loved to roam the neighborhood and play pickup sports, and he indulged in organized sports as well. His pattern was to hyper-focus on one sport for a while, quickly tire of it, and then move on. In seventh grade, he was good enough at track to go to the national tournament, where he ran the mile in five minutes! "I got tremendously good at things," Steve told me, "but I just would get bored and try something else. I didn't have anyone in my life who understood me enough to mentor me in harnessing my tremendous energy. As high school started, I became disillusioned and frustrated with school, my family, and my whole life. I was a ship lost at sea."

A trip to the wilds of the Rocky Mountains gave Steve hope that his life could be different:

> In ninth grade, my best friend and his family took me with them on a skiing vacation out West. I am not sure if it was the skiing or the mountains, but I focused better than I ever had. Something about the extreme and constant physical activity combined with the awe-inspiring beauty to make me feel at home and fully alive. I was depressed and dejected when that trip ended, but also filled with a passion to return.

Steve remembers always feeling restless. During the trip, however, that feeling temporarily retreated. "It was a miracle," he said.

When he got back home, Steve felt a strong urge to escape the stagnation and frustration he felt. He jumped at the chance to spend the summer on Lake Michigan with his best friend, whose family had a home on the water. The two of them bummed around the beach and had a great time together until an incident caused them to come to physical blows. Steve decided to leave. "The prospect of returning home, and to school, horrified me," he said. "Things had just become unbearable. At the age of fifteen, I decided to trek back to Colorado." Steve left his family and the life he knew behind.

He hitchhiked all the way to Denver, with his family unaware of his whereabouts. He lived in a dark corner of a parking garage and ate his meals at a local soup kitchen. All he had on his feet were flip-flops. After a few weeks, he was hired as a busboy. He socked away enough money after a few months to fly to Salt Lake City. He then hitchhiked to a town called Snowbird because he had heard about its incredible skiing. Steve loved it, working at a restaurant and skiing as much as he possibly could. He sacrificed many creature comforts but was happy being outside and close to nature all the time:

> I was still without housing and slept on floors, in closets, on couches, wherever I could, for the next six months. I did get in touch with my parents, and they came out to see me. I felt bad because my mom cried the whole time. I was really happy, however, because when I was not working, I could ski and be outdoors, and this outweighed everything I should have been doing. I know this was selfish. I feel guilty when I look back over the years. I have done many selfish things that allowed me to be outdoors and active at the expense of my family, parents, wife, and children. I just feel so much better physically and emotionally when I am active and outside. I am not sure how my children will feel about me later in life, and this worries me.

From Utah, Steve was drawn to a series of dangerous, if not life-threatening, occupations. Upon completing his GED—which he passed without studying and by guessing his way through—he decided to become a Marine. After two days of boot camp, he determined he was not cut out for that life and fled in the middle of the night. His parents hired a lawyer, who was able to help Steve avoid prison. After that fiasco, Steve was drawn to work on offshore oil rigs. He enrolled in a Florida diving school for commercial deep-sea construction, a program he finished in a lightning-fast six months. He quickly obtained an apprentice dive job with the largest marine construction company in the world. Steve worked offshore for three years, during which time he got married. In 1984 he was caught in Hurricane Juan and became injured and unable to dive. He moved back to Michigan, joined the carpenters' union, and worked as an apprentice carpenter for a few years until an incident in which he fell thirty-five feet from a scaffold that had collapsed. Steve spent two years recovering from his injuries, but abject boredom and immobility motivated him to finish his education. "A friend of mine was studying dentistry," Steve said, "and I loved working with my hands, so I thought it would be a good route to take."

> *Studies conclusively correlate an increased risk for serious injury with ADHD. Medication does not significantly protect against injury in ADHD patients. One study demonstrated a threefold increase in risk for skull fractures in ADHD individuals.[3] Safety should be instilled in ADHDers from a very young age.*

I am sure none of Steve's grade-school teachers would have ever thought him capable of becoming a dentist. He took a most circuitous and idiosyncratic route to his profession:

I realized that an undergraduate degree was not a prerequisite for some dental schools, so I studied for the entrance exam as if my life depended on it. There was little chance of me completing loads of boring course work, so I knew I had to take advantage of this shortcut. I did have to enroll in some prerequisite courses—which took me two years to complete—but that was a whole lot better than having to take the 120 credits needed for a degree. My struggles paid off. I was one of two applicants that year accepted to the prestigious University of Michigan Dental School without an undergraduate degree.

Dental school was a baptism of fire for Steve. "I had not really developed any study skills," he said, "so I pretty much had to study day and night." The hands-on aspect of dentistry turned out to be a great fit. His love of the instruments, devices, and tools helped keep him focused: "Knowing that the classwork was going to allow me to work with my hands in a way that interested me was the greatest source of motivation. In previous years, I had never seen the point to classwork. But every class I took in dental school had a purpose, which kept my brain on fire." In his senior year of dental school, Steve had done so well that he was accepted for an internship in a medical degree program for oral surgery. He had to turn it down at that time because his wife had become pregnant with their second child. But it was a great badge of honor for Steve that he was accepted to both dental and medical school without an undergraduate degree and without ever having taken the ACT or SAT.

Steve bought a practice once he finished dental school, and his enormous energy and great people skills allowed him to double the practice in less than ten years. While he has enjoyed great professional success, he has cut back on working because he has a daughter with ADHD, and it's more important for him to help her get what she needs. He sold his practice and moved to New Hampshire to be close to a school he believes is a great fit for her. "She's brilliant," Steve said, "but I don't want her to have to suffer like I did in order to figure that out."

Steve's story shows the destructive influence school can have for some ADHDers, but it also gives great hope that it is possible to carve out individual unique paths to happiness and fulfillment. I have seen countless loved ones create suffering for themselves and the ADHDers in their lives because they insist on traditional paths of learning and career. Not everyone is as smart and talented as Steve, but creative career paths abound. My intern, Will, a.k.a. "The Guard," never did manage to succeed in college. But he has parlayed his experience working with ADHD adolescents into an opportunity. He is a caregiver for teens with special needs. He charges twenty dollars an hour and is quite content with his earning potential. He has business cards and a brochure, and he markets his services to therapists, counselors, and teachers. He has more work than he can handle.

Will had me as an ally and advisor as he carved out his independent business, which brings to mind the importance of ADHDers getting support. Steve had a loving and understanding wife. I had—and have—a whole host of mentors. People who lack innate drive in the motivational centers of the brain usually need support to persevere.

SUPPORT. SUPPORT. SUPPORT.

Father Donoher was so impressed by my knowledge of the Bible that he began to keep me after class to discuss theology with him. I think he thought I was a good candidate for the priesthood. He called me in during Christmas break of freshman year to help him grade exams. My mother beamed with pride as she dropped me off that cold December day. The previous year, I had been deemed a likely candidate for failure, and now I was essentially a teacher's pet. My transformation was complete and I reveled in my newfound status as a smart and reliable student. Those teachers helped me access power I did not realize was within me, but I also had a secret weapon: my mother.

My mother never talked down to me. She had an unobtrusive way of offering a small suggestion and then leaving it alone, conveying to me that she didn't care whether I took her advice. It was her nonchalant demeanor that helped me to be open to what she said. I remember sitting and reading one day, my attention fading in and out. I told my mother, "I'm having a hard time staying focused, and it's really starting to frustrate me." She responded, "When I have trouble staying focused on a book, I stand up to read, and I even walk around." With that, she picked up a book, started reading, and left the room. I decided to ride the exercise bike while I read textbooks that bored me. Presto! I stayed focused, got my reading done with a lot less suffering, and lost five pounds in the process.

> *Exercise is among the best "treatments" for ADHD. It increases blood flow and the levels of important brain chemicals. With daily exercise, we naturally help ourselves pay attention to things that might bore us, and we stay on task. Exercise has also been noted for its antidepressant and antianxiety benefits.[4] When I experience writer's block, abdominal crunches are a reliable method to get me refocused. Don't skimp on physical activity!*

My mother did another brilliant thing. When she noticed that I had taken her up on a suggestion, she let it be my victory and showed no need for recognition. I often use techniques, such as that one, suggested by my mother. My mother inspired me to get creative.

Knowing my tendency to forget, I began to leave notes for myself all around the house. At one point, it got so bad that I used to have to write notes to remind myself where my notes were. But the truly effective technique was to write a note and put it in my shoe, because then when I took it off at home, out popped the note. At night, I put notes in my shoe so that I would see them the next morning before I went to school. My mother said nothing, but I would find little squares of colored paper cut out and stacked in my room and in my school bag. She quietly supported me, and when I received a 3.7 grade point average my first semester of high school, she gave me all the credit. She never failed in her belief that I would succeed.

One particularly tough subject for me was biology. My mother saw me racking my brain over the material on a certain test. She informed me, "You know, dear, I heard some salespeople talking at my Mary Kay seminar, and they said that when they really have to remember something, they make cassette tapes to study from." I immediately took to the idea. I made cassette study tapes and would listen to those as I went to bed. I had a little cassette player that I listened to while riding my bike. On Mr. Schuete's midyear biology exam, I scored the highest grade among his 160 students. I made tapes for any class that gave me trouble. This technique propelled me into the upper academic echelons. I became somewhat addicted to the success I achieved that first semester, and I didn't want to let go of it. I did anything and everything that might give me an edge.

I had charts, posters, and pictures all around my room. I started coming up with new methods on my own. My mother made me believe in myself and convinced me that every problem had a solution. She was a powerful mentor.

PERSEVERANCE

ADHDers often give up quickly. Many of us have particularly low tolerance for frustration. Steve's ultimate perseverance was created by life-threatening injuries. It took something extreme and severe to set him on his path. Similar to Steve, John had struggled for many years before he finally found his passion as an automotive designer. "I loved to draw and design," John said, "and that's what I did through most of my school years. When my hand was moving, I could pay attention." John brought his daughter, Chloe, to me when she was eleven years old. Like her father, she was an incredibly creative individual. John's mandate to me was simple: "I don't want my daughter to have to wait until she's thirty-five before she finds what she's good at." Like Steve, John had given up on school before discovering his career. "If I could have found a reason to get through college right away," John told me, "I could have accomplished so much more in my life."

When Chloe started coming to my ADHD Study Groups, she was experiencing problems across all subject areas. Having an IQ in the gifted range made her poor school performance quite difficult to bear. Her father had given her a great gift, though: from the time she was a small girl, he had continually filled her head with his belief in her abilities. He tirelessly searched for things she was good at. When she showed interest in the theater, he enrolled her in summer camps and voice lessons. He bought a video camera and started encouraging her to act in her own videos. Father and daughter designed and constructed movie sets. "I knew she was gifted, and I was desperate to preserve her belief in herself," John said. "I didn't want her to go through the decades of self-doubt that had plagued me."

Chloe's struggles in math were particularly punishing. She would memorize her multiplication tables one night, only to have the information seemingly evaporate by the next day. She would get 100 percent on a practice test that I would give her and then fail the actual test the next day. I puzzled over Chloe, sometimes staying up late devising new plans of action, most of which produced little in the way of tangible results. Surprisingly, Chloe never stopped trying. Her father's strategy had worked.

When Chloe was in eighth grade, we finally discovered one of the main culprits of her troubles: she experienced anxiety, which is very common in ADHDers, especially those with a high IQ. It was determined that she would take her tests in the school's learning resource center. This made a huge difference in all subjects except math. Her math teacher, Susan Krauss—one of the most compassionate, caring, and steadfast teachers I have ever met—suggested that for her final exam I come to school, pick up Chloe, and take her somewhere other than school. I took her to Monty's Grill, a small neighborhood restaurant with the friendliness and charm of the bar from the TV show *Cheers*. In the course of three hours, and three chocolate milk shakes, Chloe completed her exam with no help from me. She scored an 88 percent. We had changed the environment, surrounded her with creature comforts, and temporarily banished the anxiety, allowing her innate abilities to shine through. "I never seem to do things the same way as everyone else," Chloe told me recently, "but I know that I can always find a way to succeed. Taking my math test at Monty's made me believe that anything was possible." Chloe went from failing a lot of classes to all As and Bs. Her belief in herself propelled her into film school. She did an internship last summer with Pixar Studios.

Chloe could have easily given up on herself, as many ADHDers do. Perseverance must be taught and encouraged. In persevering in our belief about the ADHDers in our lives, we model perseverance for them!

INSPIRATION

The ultimate goal of a mentor is to inspire. I had plenty of inspiration during high school. For all their foibles and shortcomings, the priests and teachers I encountered motivated me to rise to the challenge. Father Baumeister, for example, didn't accept excuses. If he gave me a piece of advice that I implemented and then later reported lackluster results, he gave new marching orders.

Like many ADHD folks, I had huge issues with being careful and detail-oriented in math. I knew the material, but would forget a negative sign, fail to reduce a fraction, or carelessly multiply incorrectly. I sought Baumeister's help to solve this problem. He had me come in to school every morning. I stood at the board and worked problems he rattled off. He timed me, so I had to work quickly, and he diligently watched as I solved problems on the board, barking at me incessantly that I was "taking too damned long." At the first sign of a mistake, he would roar, "What in the hell do you think you're doing? Be careful! You can do it! Just be careful!" After a few weeks of this, my speed in doing problems noticeably increased. At that point, Baumeister said, "Kevin, the only way you're going to get As on my tests is to quickly finish them and then go back and rework each problem; if you don't get the same answer, you've probably made a mistake, and then *you fix it!*" The man made an A math student out of me, and math ceased being a problem. I owe him a lot, and it only took me twenty years to figure that out. I needed the tough love that he had to offer. I needed the intensity. General Patton once said, "When I want something to stick, I give it to 'em loud and dirty." "Boot Camp Math" worked for me. That teaching style got my brain moving, and it hasn't stopped. More than anyone before or since, Father Baumeister helped me understand my brain and made me believe in my own power to solve problems in ways that were consistent with my learning style.

I didn't have the ADHD label at that point, which I think was a blessing, because that crotchety curmudgeon of a math teacher infused me with the belief that I was a highly intelligent human being and that I *was* hardwired with the ability to solve problems and work through difficulties. He also made me realize that I would never join the army.

After that first year of hell, during which I spent three to five hours every night on homework, schoolwork became much easier for me. The strategies I had developed had worked, and during tenth through twelfth grades, I progressively got more bang for the academic buck. The struggle to invent new ways to keep focused continued, however, because once a certain method became predictable and routine, I would tire of it. But even though I struggled with peer relationships, I did feel that I was a full-fledged member of an academic community, something many ADHDers unfortunately never experience.

EMPOWERADD: BUILDING COMMUNITY

The EmpowerADD Project (www.empoweradd.org), a not-for-profit corporation, was created to give support and provide community to ADHD teens and young adults, helping them launch into successful lives by focusing on their unique strengths and talents. The organization was the brainchild of Jeff Lane, whose vision I quickly took on as my own. Lane had retired at age forty-nine from a successful and lucrative career as an executive in the automotive industry. Having experienced the impact of ADHD in his extended family, Lane found a worthy focus for his deep-seated and growing desire to "give back" to the community for the great fortune he had enjoyed. "Family is the most important thing in my life," Lane said. "I saw so many times how ADHD tore families apart. I wanted to do something that would ensure that did not happen."

Lane travelled around the country, meeting experts on ADHD and sharing his ever-expanding vision of how he thought he could help. He received support from every one of these experts after he laid out his passionate intention for creating a community for ADHD people. Discussing his vision with Ellen Wietiecha, a childhood friend, led her to suggest Lane meet me. "He's been creating an ADHD community for the last ten years," she told him.

Lane asked me why I had such a high success rate with ADHD people, referencing the fact that students who have come to ADHD Study Groups twice a week or more for four months have attained an average increase in their grade point average of 1.56 points. I told him it was simply the magic of providing a place where ADHD is the norm. "When they are free to perform in the 'ADHD mode,' they are amazingly productive," I told him.

My strengths-based approach to educating ADHD individuals resonated deeply with Lane. A strengths-based approach to ADHD views lack of success in the classroom as deriving, at least in part, from the fact that ADHD students learn differently and do not receive adequate accommodation for their differences. They, like all individuals, have unique perceptual preferences for taking in information, communicating with others, and inter-acting with the world around them.[5] Such preferences in ADHD people have, however, been viewed for the most part through the "disorder" lens. Scant attention has been given to consider-ing ADHD simply as a way of being, with its own advantages and disadvantages. Realizing the incredible need, Lane was white-hot with passion for concentrating on strengths.

He hired me to design a curriculum that would teach ADHD people about themselves from a strengths-based perspective, one that would be so engaging that participants would want to come back. This goal was not easy with a population accustomed to giving up, predisposed to boredom, and lacking in follow-through. In our first year, we had forty participants ages fifteen to twenty-five, each of whom went through eight 2.5-hour modules. We had only two absences, which in my book amounts to a stunning achievement. In a quasi-classroom setting, we taught these folks about crucial aspects of ADHD: organization, planning, addiction, neurobiology, how ADHD shows up in daily life, following through, and, most importantly, uncovering strengths.

Theoretically, the program draws on sociological and psychological research that demonstrates the efficacy of dealing with life issues in a group setting. Group activities generate greater energy, which serves to motivate and creates long-lasting momentum.[6] EmpowerADD does not seek to transmit a body of knowledge, but rather to create an atmosphere in which participants come up with their own strategies and are given latitude to make their own decisions. Shifts in attitudes and behavior come more easily when people come up with their own solutions.[7] Groups help individuals refine their ideas by challenging and simply discussing them.[8] Evidence is mounting that group processes work particularly well for ADHD people.[9]

Using MacKenzie's model of group strength,[10] the EmpowerADD Project has demonstrated a superior ability to create a cohesive group dynamic: regular and punctual attendance (only one participant stopped the program without finishing), high levels of active participation, willingness to take risks regarding new behaviors, and quick development of a shared belief in the values of the program (members readily gave and accepted feedback). The cohesiveness of the group creates safety for each participant to honestly share about his or her successes and failures. As the facilitator, I convene the groups, but they quickly take on a life of their own apart from my intervention. Peer coaching makes up a significant aspect of the program. Many studies have shown significant benefits to academic and social outcomes in ADHD individuals who are compassionately coached by their peers.[11]

Each activity is high-energy and multifaceted, with a strong dose of fun, an indispensable quality for any group containing people with ADHD.[12] Short lectures are interrupted by games, music, videos, modeling, role-playing, and comedy. I love being there with the students. They are my kind, and I "teach" in a way that allows them to effortlessly stay focused. When a few start losing focus, I realize I need to change tactics, and I do. We play-fully and joyfully tackle the challenges of ADHD. "Why wasn't school like this?" many of them ask. Interruption, boredom, the need to move around, and the need to crack jokes are accepted, not pathologized. Many of the participants feel part of a positive group for the first time in their lives. We do, however, work on taking control of behaviors that others find annoying.

One nineteen-year-old man, Alex, had filtering issues. He would often blurt out whatever came to his mind, often with very "inappropriate" subject matter. Everyone in class found him annoying, which they often expressed. Alex broke down one day in class, saying, "This is what always happens to me. I piss people off and then no one wants to be around me." One particularly astute participant, Asa, immediately chimed in, "You're like I used to be. You just don't have good filters." With that line, a light went off in my head. I quickly grabbed note cards and wrote "FILTER" on each of them, passing one out to everybody in class and instructing them that, when Alex blurted out something, not to say anything to him, but simply to raise their "FILTER" placard. Of course, I entreated them to use this device sparingly and in a non-shaming way. We made it a game and gave Alex some control over the process. He had three "challenges" per class: if he thought someone had incorrectly used the placard toward him, he could appeal to a vote from the class. If he won the challenge, the person whom he challenged had to buy him a Coke. The impact was instantaneous. We gave him the filters he did not have.

His verbal impulsivity decreased inside and outside of class. "I take you guys with me to school and work," Alex said. "It's like I don't have filters inside me, but now I have all of you."

Alex's story shows the power of building community with ADHDers. One of the great enduring gaps that ADHDers experience is a lack of community; they miss out on feeling a sense of purposeful connection with the world around them. Their early experiences teach them to skirt the margins, staying at a safe enough distance to avoid being hurt again. A safety gap is understandably erected between the ADHDer and the rest of the world. The EmpowerADD Project is filling in this gap.

> Having been peer-rejected for many years seems to predispose ADHD young people to picking deviant friends,[13] a fact that further increases the risks for substance abuse, criminal behavior, and a host of psychological and social difficulties. Creating positive friendships at an early age is of paramount importance.[14]

The evidence for the success of EmpowerADD is not just anecdotal. Each participant takes a self-efficacy questionnaire before and after the program. In every measure we examine, the program has made an improvement in the extent to which the participants feel able to meet life's challenges. Measures of motivation, adaptability, and self-regulation all increase over the course of the eight-week program. More data need to be collected, but the most amazing thing is that the effect seems stronger when we question them six months after completing the program. Not surprisingly, this effect is greater in participants who came back and trained to be staff!

Ross came to EmpowerADD with a 1.5 grade point average during his junior year of high school. Six months later, he was pulling a 3.4. "EmpowerADD taught me how my mind worked," Ross said. "I use my phone for reminders, study in short bursts, and I now know that I need to have fun to keep myself energized. I also realized that part of my not caring about school was about me sort of being angry at the world. Kevin and Jeff helped to get to the bottom of this problem and to let go of my anger." We are finding that with intense support and understanding, ADHDers do succeed. They just need to find their own unique path.

PLAYING WITH FIRE

EmpowerADD caters significantly to young men, a good many of whom could be called what I dub "gun-and-knife-show" ADHDers. They love weapons, fire, and blowing stuff up. I know it is easy to cringe at such a characterization, but if we did not have people like this, who would put out our forest and oil-well fires? Where would we find intrepid individuals to create fire-works and organize explosive extravaganzas for the Fourth of July? Who would experimentally start and study fires to further our knowledge of arson? Who would don a thermal suit and brave hellish temperatures and toxic gas to work as a hands-on volcanologist? One of my former ADHD students is actually working in that field!

In prehistoric societies, of course, giftedness with fire would have guaranteed a place of honor in the tribe. Those of us at the EmpowerADD Project seek to uncover a place of honor for every ADHDer who comes through our doors. One brilliant nineteen-year-old, Brett, had conned his way through high school, getting parents and tutors to do most of his homework and charming teachers into continually cutting him slack. His tricks stopped working in college, and he flunked out. My inner con man was not fooled by him, and I spent the eight weeks of our course hammering and haranguing him every day. I relentlessly called and texted him and chatted with him on Facebook. "You can't bullshit a bullshitter," I told him. "I'm a liar in recovery, so you're not going to be able to lie to me." I saw a great deal of myself in Brett, and I wondered if I might have ended up in the same predicament had I not had such powerful mentors who pierced through my trickery.

After he completed the EmpowerADD program, Brett became an intern at my ADHD Study Groups. Helping others do their schoolwork stimulated Brett to do his own. He had a particular gift with two fourteen-year-old boys, Todd and Stefan, whom I had struggled to engage. Brett and these two boys all carried around lighters, even though none of them smoked. They had that penchant for fire that I have seen so often in ADHD males. On one occasion, I had some candles I was going to throw away, and one of the boys stopped me and asked if they could have them. I agreed. The next time they were all together, I found them burning candles and then dumping the liquefied wax into various containers. They were trying to make their own candles, and they also made a huge mess. They started bringing over candles of their own, and I was just about ready to ban candles when I had an idea. If life gives you wax, why not make candles? A business was born!

When I suggested they should start a candle-making business, they all got very excited. Todd researched supplies, and the other two worked on techniques. They went together to a candle-making demonstration at Greenfield Village, a local historical museum. They decided to start with beeswax and settled on a few simple molds. Using Facebook for marketing, they have sold forty to fifty candle packages per month in their first few months. Stefan designed the packaging. They have capitalized on a fascination with fire. These three ADHDers naturally excel in creativity and marketing, and they love working with their hands. Finding each other allowed them to find a common passion. Their focus on the project has its ups and downs, but they have persisted. "This is one of the first really good things I have ever done," Todd said. "I'm starting to believe I can be a success." I have no doubt that all three will expand their present business and create others down the road. ADHDers make great entrepreneurs. Incidentally, the three young men brought in Brett's sister to do their accounting. Brett put in practice a lesson from EmpowerADD when he asked for help for something he struggled with.

I am convinced that the EmpowerADD Project helps level the playing field by focusing on its participants' talents and gifts. ADHD people come to a place where their way of being is the norm. For perhaps the first time in their lives, they are in an environment in which they can succeed just by totally and authentically being who they are. There is little conflict for them at EmpowerADD. Jeff Lane and I believe that we are training an army of entrepreneurs, innovators, and creators. We not only have a mission to help ADHD people, but we also believe that by empowering their tremendous untapped potential, we are doing a great service to the human race.

HEALING FAMILIES

ADHD can take a toll on families. As part of our work with the EmpowerADD Project, we invite parents, spouses, and significant others to learn about ADHD by learning first about themselves. Before coming to their first session, the participants take two strengths-oriented assessments. The Kolbe assessment measures how humans complete tasks based on instinct. We have found that people who come to EmpowerADD have high levels of instinctual responses that lend themselves to creativity, innovation, design, and building. They also typically have low levels of instincts related to fact-finding, organization, follow-through, and risk assessment. (Interestingly, teachers are typically the exact opposite!) Participants also take the Process Communication Personality Inventory. We focus on ADHDers' unique ways of communicating and taking in information, and how they stay energized. We view their personality and task-oriented instincts as valid and encourage them to honor who they are in every decision they make. Our strengths-based assessment tools provide a common language that helps us begin the process of viewing ADHD as a set of predispositions and not a life-limiting pathology.

Families of our participants also come and take these assessments. We use the results as the starting point for a day-long intensive training for parents, siblings, and significant others on how to relate to their ADHD loved one. We find that many of the parents and spouses have instinctual and personality profiles that put them into conflict with their ADHD loved one. We also find that understanding each other's instincts regarding solving a problem and regarding ADHDers' perceptual and interactive preferences has the power to lessen conflict and heal relationships. We model the wisdom of Dr. Kathy Kolbe: "Successful people are those who have found paths that allow them to use their instinctive powers freely without stepping on others."[15] Our family trainings help to lessen conflict by inviting everyone in the family to appreciate each other's strengths and innate preferences. Interpersonal obstacles are overcome by attaining greater understanding of oneself, which serves as a template to then appreciate the unique differences of others.

A LIFE'S WORK

The EmpowerADD Project is the culmination of my life's work. Several folks who have attended and observed the sessions have asked me how I designed such a unique program. I tell them that it is not so much that I designed a program, but that I have received the gift of a platform, a stage on which the lessons I've learned about myself and ADHD can come out.

I started life with a mother, two sisters, and scores of their friends who appreciated me. I entertained them and made them laugh. I have very early memories of the adults in my life frequently complimenting me by saying things like "Did you hear what he said yesterday?" I felt I was very special. School significantly subverted that feeling of specialness. After I was told by a nun at school that I was "not following God's plan," my mother consoled me with a line that still remains within me: "God has something very special in mind for you."

The support and creativity of my family underlie my success in surmounting social and academic obstacles. They indelibly infused me with the belief that I had the power to solve in my own way every problem I encountered. I was constantly reaffirmed, which served as a potent balance to the negative messages that seeped in from school and even from my peers. My mother and sisters helped me devise creative strategies to move past every barrier that blocked my progress. In spite of their steadfastness, I still had a great deal of work to do as an adult, as I went about the task of figuring out how to have a career and a life as an ADHDer in a non-ADHD world.

I had only been exposed to one career model, which held that a successful individual found one thing he or she did well and stuck with it. My grandmother reminded me of my grandfather's embodiment of this principle: "He worked for McNaughton-McKay for forty-seven years and never missed a day of work." I wanted to live up to my grandmother's expectation. I tried to continue teaching school, but being tied to a few subject areas in one small room for seven hours day after day, year after year, quickly came to feel like a prison, so I escaped. Other jobs followed, with each one quickly turning into tedium.

When the parent of one of my former pupils asked me to help her son succeed in school, I assumed it would be just a temporary stopover on the road to finding a fulfilling, lucrative career. I never dreamed that I would be loving this vocational adventure thirteen years later, let alone writing a book about it!

In helping other ADHDers, I help myself every single day. Dealing with the challenges of organization, motivation, planning, and follow-through in my clients stimulates me to constantly work on those things in myself. The people I see professionally help me just as much as I help them. For this reason, I have come to believe that ADHDers need to volunteer in the community. By helping others, our self-esteem and effectiveness increase. To graduate from the EmpowerADD Project, participants must do a community service project. One of my favorites involved a group called Blight Busters (www.blightbusters.org) that helps tear down abandoned houses in Detroit and then works toward beautifying and revitalizing neighborhoods. Our graduates have participated in demolishing houses and carting away the debris, as well as painting, repairing, gardening, and building maintenance. Feeling like they have something to give energizes and motivates them. Seeing five energized ADHDers with sledge hammers was an amazing experience. "Where did you find these guys?" the site manager asked. "This is one of the best volunteer crews we have ever had."

I like to mention the Blight Busters event because it shows in concrete terms the great impact ADHDers can have in the community. I have come to believe that the work I do is less about helping ADHD people and more about empowering them to help humanity by simply doing what they do best.

If you take anything away from this book, understand that what you see as weakness could very well be strength. Arm yourself with awareness, an arsenal of creative tools, and a belief in the power of the ADHD mind. Assume that the ADHDer in your life was put on this earth to help people. Take a step into the odyssey of helping him or her discover purpose, power, and potential in ADHD.

APPENDIX

THE MYSTERY OF THE ADHD BRAIN

"The temptation to form premature theories upon insufficient data is the bane of our profession."
Sherlock Holmes

ADHD EXPERTS

I go to the same coffee shop almost every morning. It is a lively place filled with constant debate and diverse opinions on a variety of issues. I find the environment quite stimulating and enjoyable, except when people offer half-baked theories on ADHD. I still struggle with the fact that many people presume to understand a disorder that for me still carries a great many unknowns.

Coffee-shop debates often require me to step in and set the record straight on ADHD in a variety of areas: ADHD is not the result of bad parenting; ADHD is not "caused" by too much sugar in the diet;[1] ADHD is not the result of laziness. It is easy to find Internet websites that claim to have the "cure" for ADHD, and people at the coffee shop regularly bring me printouts of these cyber crackpots for my perusal. One particularly annoying customer, Gerard, brings me frequent updates from online conspiracy theorists who accuse the "pharmaceutical-medical-industrial complex" of overmedicating children for profit. Gerard and his cadre of Internet gurus offer vitamins, herbs, and strange diets as viable treatments for ADHD. "If you would just be reasonable and listen to them," he often yells in my ear, "we could save the world from much needless suffering." I must admit that even I have been taken in by the occasional Internet huckster purporting to offer an easy fix to the problem. Yet, as I have researched the mystery of ADHD, I have come to the conclusion that what we *do not* know about this condition outweighs what we *do* know.

Although this appendix is rooted in contemporary scientific research, I hope it will provide the reader with an easy-to-understand description of the neurobiological nature of ADHD. I assume that a considerable amount of misinformation and misunderstanding regarding the disorder derives from a lack of knowledge of how the brain works and how the brain affects the troubling behaviors that are part of ADHD. The brain is an incredibly complex organ that is still only partially understood. Keeping this in mind, definitive conclusions are not possible at this stage of scientific research. With regard to ADHD, however, multiple streams of research point to brain differences as a basis for uncovering the roots of a condition that describes multiple behavioral profiles. But many mysteries remain.

DIAGNOSIS

ADHD is a remarkably diverse disorder that likely involves several distinct causal pathways. The prevalence of ADHD diagnoses varies from culture to culture, being diagnosed most frequently in the United States, in an estimated 8 percent of children ages 4–17 and in 2.9 to 4.4 percent of adults.[2] European and other developed nations use more stringent criteria for diagnosing the disorder, a fact that largely accounts for the discrepancy in cross-cultural diagnostic frequency. Some Internet crackpots still misuse the varying rates of ADHD in different countries as "proof" that it is overdiagnosed in the United States. I, however, believe that the condition is still underdiagnosed.

Diagnosis is presently based on behavioral signs, although some researchers envision brain scanning and measurement techniques being involved in the process in the future. There is no brain scan or blood test that can determine whether someone has the disorder. People are labeled as having ADHD according to guidelines set forth in the DSM-IV diagnostic manual, based on meeting six of nine criteria from two separate clusters of symptoms, one relating to inattention and the other to hyperactivity-impulsivity. Some people meet six or more criteria in both clusters. The three subtypes of ADHD derive from these criteria: predominantly inattentive, predominantly hyperactive-impulsive, and the combined subtype. There has been some talk about calling the inattentive subtype a distinct disorder. In fact, many people already do this by differentiating between ADD and ADHD.

Symptoms of Inattention

- Often fails to give close attention to details or makes careless mistakes.

- Often has difficulty sustaining attention in tasks or play activities.

- Often does not seem to listen when spoken to directly.

- Frequently does not follow through on instructions.

- Often has difficulty organizing tasks and activities.

- Characteristically avoids, seems to dislike, and is reluctant to engage in tasks that require sustained mental effort.

- Frequently loses objects necessary for tasks or activities.

- Is often easily distracted by extraneous stimuli.

- Is often forgetful in daily activities, chores, and running errands.

Symptoms of Hyperactivity/Impulsivity

- Often fidgets or taps hands or feet or squirms in seat.

- Is often restless during activities when others are seated.

- Often runs about or climbs on furniture and moves excessively in inappropriate situations.

- Is often excessively loud or noisy during play, leisure, or social activities.

- Is often "on the go," acting as if "driven by a motor." Is uncomfortable being still for an extended time, as in restaurants, meetings, etc.

- Often talks excessively.

- Has difficulty waiting his or her turn or waiting in line.

- Often blurts out an answer before a question has been completed. Older adolescents or adults may complete people's sentences and "jump the gun" in conversations.

- Often interrupts or intrudes on others.

- Tends to act without thinking, such as starting tasks without adequate preparation or avoiding reading or listening to instructions.

- Is uncomfortable doing things slowly and systematically and often rushes through activities or tasks.

- Finds it difficult to resist temptations or opportunities, even if it means taking risks.

Generally, some symptoms must have been present before seven years of age, and impairment must be present in at least two settings (school and home, for example). There must be clear evidence of interference with developmentally appropriate social, academic, or occupational functioning. Behavioral criteria are assessed primarily through the use of questionnaires completed by the individual, family members, and teachers in the case of schoolchildren, along with interviews and often neuropsychological testing with a clinician. Additional assessments are often employed as part of screening for ADHD, some with a view toward differential diagnosis—since ADHD shares symptoms with a variety of other conditions—and others to evaluate whether comorbid conditions, such as oppositional-defiant disorder and anxiety, present alongside ADHD.

IS IT ALL IN YOUR HEAD?

Although behavioral symptoms form the standard for diagnosis, evidence continues to mount that ADHD correlates with differences in size, structure, and functioning of the individual's neurobiological environment.

> *When I say* neurobiological environment, *I am referring to the dimensions, shape, structure, and chemical makeup of the brain and nervous system. Just as there are huge differences in climate and environments around the world, there are meaningful and important differences in the brains of ADHD and non-ADHD people.*

Genetic studies highlight, for example, patterns of inheritance that correlate with ADHD. Family studies, especially among adoptees, show a high association between some symptoms of ADHD and an individual's biological parents and siblings. Ongoing examination of specific human genes has found several polymorphisms that appear in much higher frequency among ADHD individuals, although each polymorphism is generally thought to produce only a small effect, which therefore suggests that ADHD derives from the combined effect of variations of many genes.

Research is mounting that development of ADHD arises from an interaction between the environment and genetic predispositions. Environmental factors such as prenatal trauma, lead and mercury exposure, and head injuries can greatly contribute to

ADHD. People with some developmental disorders such as spina bifida, sickle cell anemia, and cerebral palsy also seem to carry a greater risk for developing ADHD.[3] Although environmental contributors to ADHD are an important area of study, the rest of this chapter is devoted to how differences in the brain explain the symptoms of the disorder.

> A polymorphism, from the Greek poly meaning "many" and morph meaning "shape," simply refers to different forms or "shapes" of a gene. Polymorphisms are essentially DNA sequence variations that are relatively common in the population. Mutations, on the other hand, are sequence variations that are uncommon.

Many of the variations uncovered so far relate to genes that code for the structure and function of receptors and transporters of the neurotransmitter dopamine. Several other neurochemicals have also been implicated. Since many of the most successful medications used to treat ADHD are known to act on certain dopamine-related systems in the brain, much scientific effort continues to be focused on the role of these "neurological loops" in the disorder. In addition to atypical functioning and structure of these systems, overall volume of certain cerebral regions is often decreased in ADHD individuals, and underactivity, as well as reduced blood flow, have been noted in many areas of the brain that are known to be involved in "executive functions" and arousal, which are both impaired in ADHD. Deficiencies in executive functions make living a successful life very difficult. Executive functions include these:

- Working memory and recall (holding facts in mind; accessing facts stored in long-term memory)

- Activation, arousal, and effort (getting started; paying attention; finishing work)

- Controlling emotions (ability to tolerate frustration; thinking before acting or speaking)

- Internalizing language (using "self-talk" to control one's behavior and direct future actions)

- Taking an issue apart, analyzing the pieces, reconstituting the issue and organizing it into new ideas (complex problem solving)[4]

In addition to troubles in these vital areas, brain wave assessments also show atypical patterns in ADHD people. The brains of ADHD individuals exhibit distinct and significant differences that underpin behavioral manifestations of the disorder.

Attention is the ability to routinely filter vast amounts of information around us at all times, but there are several different kinds of attention. The alerting and arousal functions of attention are those that get the brain prepared to take action and keep it on a functional standby; this is the type of attention that is generally most impaired in ADHD. Interestingly, in ADHD, sustained attention does not generally seem impaired. Impairment is in the ability to start "paying full attention" from the very beginning of a task. ADHD children often react slowly in tasks that require decisive action, and they often react impulsively on tasks that require waiting.[5]

Understanding the neurobiological environment of the ADHD brain has great utility and importance, not just for scientists and clinicians, but also for the general public. Society does not demand that a wheelchair-bound person climb flights of stairs every day, yet ADHD people are regularly expected to undertake tasks they are not cerebrally suited to perform and are often scolded when they are unable to do so. While ADHD individuals regularly exert great effort to accommodate the requirements of society, little reciprocation takes place for the most part. The behavioral symptoms of ADHD are often presumed to derive from lack of willpower, laziness, psychological dysfunction, and even improper child-rearing methods, thus imposing on ADHD people assumptions of inadequacy that damage self-esteem. The damage to self-esteem and self-efficacy is often the most serious "side effect" that occurs with ADHD individuals. Learning about the brain's crucial involvement in ADHD has the potential to foster greater understanding and compassion—and thus decrease prejudice—by informing on the compelling neurobiological foundations characteristic of the condition.

HEREDITY

Research indicates a strong hereditary component in ADHD.[6] Although a significant role also seems to be exerted by the environment—how one grows up—one's genetic inheritance plays a serious and prominent role.

ADHD is a polygenic disorder, meaning that many genes combine to produce the behavioral effects.[7] Unlike Down syndrome or Huntington disease, each individual genetic variation associated with ADHD exerts a relatively small impact.[8] At some point, combined genetic variations cross a threshold that substantially increases an individual's risk for developing ADHD. Many individuals carry some genetic variants associated with ADHD and exhibit some of its symptoms. At the coffee shop, people regularly tell me things like "I have trouble remembering appointments too. But look at me; I'm successful." Yes, many people fall somewhere on the ADHD spectrum and thus have some of the traits. However, diagnosis of the condition requires meeting at least six of the nine criteria in one or both symptom clusters. It is rather common for people to exhibit multiple ADHD symptoms without their profile rising to the level of clinical diagnosis. This is significant when considering heredity, because research has shown that ADHD symptoms and associated behaviors—apart from clinical diagnosis—run in families. In families in which at least one member has ADHD, the non-ADHD siblings frequently show some behavioral traits and even genetic variations associated with the disorder, an association that holds strongly even if the siblings grow up in different environments, as in the case of adoption. Non-ADHD siblings carry a stronger likelihood of struggling with some of the same motor-control deficits, for example, that are often seen in those diagnosed with ADHD.[9] Similarity between affected and non-affected siblings has also been noted in executive functions.[10] Although some of these similarities could, and do, result from growing up in the same environment, shared brain differences derive most often from a shared genetic profile. Reductions in cortical gray matter in the brain—long associated with ADHD—have been seen in high numbers among affected and non-affected family members.[11] The 7-repeat allele—an alternate form of the dopamine receptor D4 (DRD4) gene—has been associated with poor performance on measures of intelligence, color naming, interference control, and working memory among ADHD children and their siblings.[12]

An allele is one of several forms that a gene can take. For example, there are three alleles for blood types A, B, and O. The word allele *is a shortened form of the word* allelomorph, *which itself comes from Greek and simply means "other form."*

A variation in DAT1, a gene that codes for a dopamine transporter, has exhibited strong associations with ADHD and seems to correlate with how individuals respond to medication for the disorder.[13] This gene's variant also shows up in significantly higher proportions in families in which at least one member has ADHD.[14] The word *associated* does not mean that alternate forms of the gene cause these deficits, but rather that a strong connection has been observed. The brain is an incredibly complex organ whose workings are difficult to fully comprehend, but what seems important is that many studies have identified genetic variations that are common to ADHD people and their non-diagnosed siblings.

Studies continue to confirm that having an ADHD relative increases an individual's risk that he or she will also have the condition. In one striking study, 84 children were identified as at risk for developing the condition. The rate of ADHD in children in this study whose parents also had the disorder was 75 percent.[15] Although this data is significantly higher than other findings, studies show that between 10 and 35 percent of immediate family members of ADHD individuals also have the condition; siblings of ADHD individuals have an approximate 30 percent chance of having the disorder.[16] ADHD runs in families, and this fact seems to derive to a significant extent from shared genetic traits, which then code for cerebral dysfunctions that ultimately, with some input from the environment, produce the symptoms of ADHD.

END BEHAVIORS AND NEUROCHEMISTRY

Children with ADHD have a considerably higher rate of missing or duplicated DNA segments compared to unaffected children, and there is a demonstrated genetic link between these segments and other brain disorders.[17] These findings from a 2010 study add even more credibility to the genetic link to ADHD. While inheritance patterns and gene variants among family members also point to genetic involvement, they do not explain the mechanisms by which ADHD is ultimately expressed. In scientific terms, the genotype—the particular sequences of genes or forms of a gene—codes for how the brain is built, which then interacts with environmental factors that give rise to the expression of ADHD symptoms or traits. This idea underpins a broad swath of contemporary understandings of the disorder and the direction of much of the current research.

Many recent studies have focused on identifying ADHD endophenotypes, intermediate dysfunctions that lie somewhere between the genetic makeup and the end behavior, or trait, called simply the phenotype. For example, difficulty following through on tasks is a symptom, or characteristic, of ADHD, and poor working memory can be viewed as the underlying endophenotype that is largely responsible. The 7-repeat allele of the DRD4 gene, a genotypic factor, has been associated with poor working memory, although this association does not represent anything close to a complete understanding of the mechanisms involved. Rather, it simply underscores the complex nature of ADHD, and provides evidence for some underlying genetic involvement.

Phenotype: *The outward expression or physical trait, such as brown eyes versus blue eyes or being able to easily sit still versus being fidgety.* Pheno *means showing or appearing.*

Genotype: *The DNA blueprint that codes for these traits. Your genetic "blueprint" determines what traits, or phenotypes, you end up with.*

Endophenotype: *An inherited trait that is associated with a condition, but not a direct symptom.*

For example, the ability to delay an impulse, or wait, is impaired in ADHD, and is, in fact, a diagnostic criterion. This would be considered a phenotype, an apparent behavior. Damage to the caudate nucleus (a part of the basal ganglia associated with learning, memory, and motor control) in the brain seems to relate to the inability to strategically wait, which might be called impulsivity. This would be the endophenotype. The genotype would be the sequences of DNA that coded for the atypical development/structure of the caudate. Incidentally, damage to the caudate, as seen in victims of trauma, has been strongly associated with impulsivity.[18]

To expand understanding of ADHD, scientists have been trying to clarify the interaction between genotype, endophenotype, and end behavior (phenotype). Appreciating correlations with gene variants is only part of the picture. There is a chain that proceeds from one's genes (how they interact with each other and the external environment) to how those interactions produce meaningful differences in the individual that lead to ADHD. Although research into illuminating the steps along this chain is quite young, two genes that correlate to ADHD have been considerably investigated: DAT1, a dopamine transporter gene, and DRD4, a dopamine receptor gene.

> *To appreciate the significance of these genes in ADHD requires some knowledge of the neurotransmitter dopamine. Dopamine systems are involved heavily in reward, in shifting attention, and in movement. Dopamine pathways in the brain are known to be impaired in addiction-prone individuals. Schizophrenia involves too much dopamine, whereas too little is implicated in Parkinson's disease. Higher levels of dopamine are associated with creativity.[19]*

Many behaviors that are deficient in ADHD individuals can be considered dopamine dependent; that is to say, several ADHD symptoms derive at least in part from deficiencies in how dopamine operates within the brain. This deficiency is thought to be a significant operating factor in the brain that ultimately ends up producing symptoms.

DOPAMINE AND ADHD

Neurons, or nerve cells, meet at "junctions" called synapses. For an impulse to travel through the brain effectively—and thus lead to desired actions and behaviors—it must cross this synapse from one neuron to another. To cross this gap requires help from a neurotransmitter. Dopamine, a versatile neuro-compound, is one such neurotransmitter—though certainly not the only one—that is particularly crucial to carrying out many of the behaviors that remain deficient in ADHD. Dopamine neuron activity is essential for cerebral processing that requires planning as well as "goal-directed behavior," two functions that require evaluation of predicted outcomes, and thus engagement of motivation to take action to achieve those outcomes.[20] These dopamine-dependent functions are frequently impaired in ADHD people.

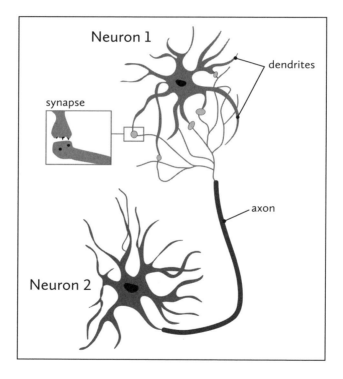

Dopamine levels increase in a part of the brain called the nucleus accumbens during the "anticipatory phase" of goal-driven behavior. Dopamine levels "are at their highest when an animal is actively seeking food, a safe place, or a mate."[21] When we learn that a blizzard is on its way, we stock up on supplies and necessities. As animals perceive the onset of cooler weather, they busy themselves—under the influence of elevated dopamine levels—collecting food or preparing their winter dens. Animals anticipate a future crisis and take action, with the help of dopamine, to guide their behavior in a way that will avert the crisis.

Dopamine is integrally involved in a variety of functions including movement, regulation of blood flow and hormone levels, and setting the timing of the movement of the intestines.[22] In ADHD, dopamine's involvement in learning is one of the most crucial elements. Several studies suggest that dopamine neuron activity acts as an internal reward signal, or "teaching signal," that helps to acquire habits in tasks with delayed reinforcement, especially those that require planning.[23] Tripp and Wickens surveyed the literature regarding the role of dopamine systems in ADHD and have proposed, based on available research, a theory they call the Dopamine Transfer Deficit (DTD), which theoretically accounts for many, though not all, of ADHD's deficiencies.[24] Again, research into this area is just beginning, but many studies replicate the existence of several dopamine-related genes in ADHD, making it one of the few psychiatric disorders with replicated genetic discoveries.[25]

Learning relates to reinforcement and reward, and as any parent of an ADHD child will attest, reinforcing positive (desired) behaviors does not always produce good results with that child. ADHD children consistently choose immediate, small rewards over delayed but larger ones.[26] Sitting still, taking notes, and listening to the teacher, for example, are behaviors with little immediate gratification, but offer significant longer-term rewards such as higher grades, positive teacher evaluation, and parental esteem. ADHD children in the classroom will often prefer short-term reinforcement like joking and playing to get the attention of classmates or looking out the window to find a source of stimulation that provides immediate reinforcement. In non-ADHD children, the experience of praise for good grades and reports will lead, at the cellular level, to a type of phasic dopamine release that relates to anticipating a future reward, and this anticipation makes enough dopamine available in the brain to keep the child focused, on task, and behaving "appropriately" in the classroom. This "anticipatory" release of dopamine seems to be deficient in ADHD individuals.[27] Classroom behaviors that get ADHD children in trouble often derive, to a significant extent, from deficiencies in the brain's basic dopaminergic systems.[28] In ADHD individuals, longer-term reward potential does not produce the release of dopamine needed to sustain alertness and focus in many low-intensity situations.

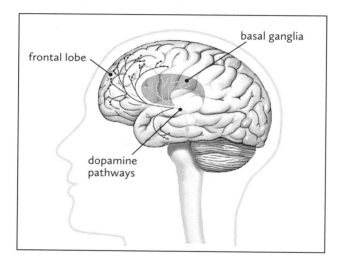

Dopamine input in the region of the brain called the basal ganglia is crucial to its reward-related learning functions.[29] The caudate and the putamen, located in this region, assist with motor control, motivation, and executive functions, and these cerebral areas are closely interconnected with the prefrontal cortices.[30] The basal ganglia, particularly the striatal areas, and the prefrontal cortices are also reduced in size in ADHD individuals, causing patterns of underactivation, especially while performing "executive" tasks.[31] Researchers have identified five neural loops between the prefrontal cortices and the basal ganglia that, in addition to the above-mentioned functions, also seem important in motivation, behavioral control, and emotional response.[32] While many studies suggest lowered levels of dopamine—and overall impairment of dopaminergic systems—in the prefrontal cortex of ADHD individuals,[33] animal studies have shown that increased neurotransmission of dopamine in the striatal (part of the basal ganglia) regions leads to hyperactivity,[34] which can also be a problem in ADHD. Some of the most basic functions of the brain's dopamine systems seem to be impaired in ADHD. Converging streams of evidence support this view.

Regarding the genetic basis of ADHD, several genes are known to be involved with the brain's dopamine systems. Some of these gene variants have been extensively studied and found to have strong associations with the symptoms of ADHD. The prefrontal cortices and basal ganglia, for example, are heavily innervated with dopamine receptors, and certain ADHD candidate genes (e.g., DAT1 and DRD4) are related to striatal and/or dorsolateral prefrontal activity that is predictive of diminished patience.[35] DAT1 is important in the reuptake (metabolism) of dopamine at the synapse, which then regulates the neural transmission of dopamine.[36] DRD4 is more involved with structures of the prefrontal cortex and is associated with faulty efficiency in the dopamine networks in that area of the brain.[37] Many genes are involved with ADHD, but evidence has certainly come together regarding the important role of dopamine-related gene variants in the disorder.

NEUROCHEMICALS AND MEDICATION

To further appreciate this picture, one can consider the success of stimulant medications. Although research into the action mechanisms of these drugs is still in the early stages, findings suggest that these medications function as dopamine-reuptake inhibitors and act on other neurotransmitters as well.[38] It is well-established that stimulant medications alter the transmission of dopaminergic neurons in the central nervous system.[39] They increase the availability of dopamine in the neural synapses, thus making transmission of dopamine-dependent neural signals more efficient. Joel Nigg posits that these psychostimulant medications may work by "enhancing the value of rewards (reinforcers) through dopamine release in the prefrontal cortices."[40] With rewards more powerful, the individual can be motivated by less immediate reward possibilities, and thus exert greater control over behavior in the moment. More than two hundred studies conducted on psychostimulants in treating ADHD show that roughly three-fourths of treated patients experience improvement in their symptoms. Strong improvements occur across a variety of ADHD symptoms: impulsivity, disruptiveness, noncompliance, talking out of turn, out-of-seat behaviors, restlessness, and even aggression.[41] Scientists believe that much of the improvement with these medications occurs because of the impact they have on the dopaminergic systems that do not function optimally in ADHD individuals.

Norepinephrine, along with dopamine, is also recognized as exerting a large role in attention, focus, motor activity, executive functions, and motivation, all of which can be impaired in ADHD.[42]

> Howard calls norepinephrine a "printer" that fixes information into long-term memory.[43] When rats are deprived of norepinephrine, for example, they can learn, but cannot remember. Norepinephrine, also called noradrenaline, is also related to activities that require drive and motivation, both of which can be impaired in ADHD.

This neurochemical, which is actually synthesized from dopamine in the body, is also involved in the body's fight-or-flight response, being released in large amounts during moments of intense shock, anger, or fear, which helps explain why memories of such events often remain vivid.[44] Studies suggest that norepinephrine is highly involved in keeping a person alert,[45] another cerebral function often impaired in ADHD. ADHD individuals have no trouble staying alert in activities that are highly stimulating, but struggle progressively as stimulation intensity decreases.[46] Although not as widely studied in ADHD, norepinephrine is now understood to act on many neuronal receptors that were once thought to be acted on solely by dopamine. Methylphenidate—also known as Ritalin, one of the most widely researched psychostimulants—increases the bioavailability of not only dopamine but also norepinephrine. Tricyclic and some other antidepressants are also thought to act on dopamine and norepinephrine, and they are used for ADHD people in whom stimulants do not work, or for whom they cause troubling side effects. Atomoxetine, also known as Strattera, is a specific norepinephrine reuptake inhibitor. This drug has been shown to greatly improve many of the symptoms of ADHD, a fact that seems to underscore the importance of norepinephrine in the condition.[47] Antihypertensive medications prescribed for ADHD, such as Clonidine, are also thought to act on the brain's noradrenergic systems.[48] Similar to the research done on the relation of dopaminergic gene variants and ADHD, recent studies confirm that some variants in noradrenergic genes correlate with ADHD as well.[49] Other neurochemicals also appear to be involved in the disorder, but much research still needs to be done. High levels of gamma-aminobutyric acid (GABA), for example, appear to correlate with some of the aggressive tendencies that can show up in ADHD[50] and relate to the ability to "dampen unwanted neural activation" and inhibit impulses.[51] Also, GABA has been linked to working memory problems.[52] Research into the neurochemical idiosyncrasies linked to ADHD is ongoing.

Although the whole picture is far from understood, research clearly indicates atypical neurochemical environments in ADHD individuals that are often improved with medications that target them. Certain gene variants that code for neurochemical pathways are increasingly found to correlate with ADHD. Some of these pathways have been repeatedly found to correlate with specific impairments that are symptoms of ADHD. Appreciating the neurobiological underpinnings of ADHD starts with the basic axiom that the roots of the atypical behavioral profiles found in ADHD individuals derive from genetic variations in the majority of cases of ADHD. These variations seem to affect the functioning of the neurochemical environment in a way that gives rise to the symptoms of the disorder. Genetic variants, for example, correlate with alterations in the dopaminergic and noradrenergic systems. These altered pathways seem to lead to dysfunctions in executive functions, alertness, learning, and motivation, among other difficulties.

Environmental factors do play a role in the way that ADHD symptoms manifest, and certainly in how ADHD children perceive themselves, and thus in how well they feel equipped to handle the challenges of life. Injuries, illness, and exposure to certain toxins can also lead to the appearance of ADHD symptoms, or exacerbate ones that preexisted.[53] However, mounds of converging evidence highlight the cerebral signature of ADHD, pointing to a disorder of the neurochemical and structural environments of the brain.

STRUCTURAL AND FUNCTIONAL ABNORMALITIES IN THE ADHD BRAIN

Neurochemical pathways seem to be impaired in ADHD; however, measurable differences in the structure of the brain have also been associated with the disorder. Functional magnetic resonance imaging (fMRI) studies have documented a somewhat decreased overall brain size of about 3 to 5 percent in patients with ADHD compared to controls[54] and a 10 to 12 percent reduction in volume of key structures in the prefrontal cortices, basal ganglia, and cerebellum.[55] It should be mentioned that many neuroimaging studies have lacked appropriate controls and have suffered from methodological problems. While the present state of technology does not allow us to peer deeply into the brain, there is enough data to assert a decreased cortical thickness as strongly associated with ADHD,[56] and several studies show a variety of anatomical abnormalities in the basal ganglia.

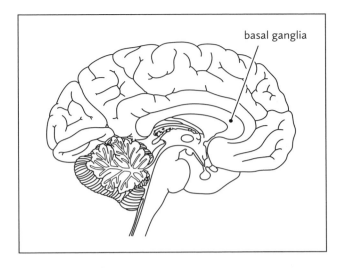

basal ganglia

Gray matter reduction in the right putamen/globus pallidus region is supported by several studies.[57] Interestingly, lesions in the right putamen have been specifically associated with ADHD symptoms after closed-head injuries in children who had not previously exhibited such symptoms,[58] providing a clear and compelling link between ADHD symptoms and abnormalities in the brain. In one study, boys with ADHD showed significantly smaller basal ganglia volumes in comparison with typical-developing boys, as well as significant differences in basal ganglia shapes.[59] The parts of the basal ganglia that showed the most significant shape differences in boys in this study are those that are known to be intricately involved with parts of the brain involved in a variety of motor and executive functions that are deficient in ADHD.[60] These "control loops" are heavily innervated with dopamine and norepinephrine receptors, a point that should help to show how much of this data converges. The fact that multiple control loops were implicated also highlights the complex nature of ADHD and the multiple causal pathways involved. Further, girls in the above-mentioned study did not show statistically significant deformities in the basal ganglia, a fact that gives evidence for gender-based differences in the disorder.

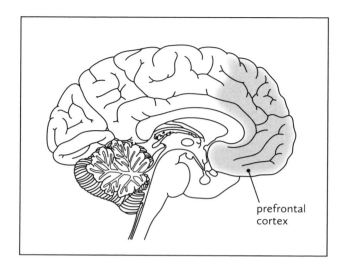

prefrontal
cortex

The frontal part of the brain called the prefrontal-striatal net-work appears smaller in ADHD individuals, especially the right side.[61] As previously mentioned, the prefrontal cortex, which is part of this network, exhibits abnormalities in the ADHD brain. When people suffer injuries to this part of the brain, a variety of the same executive function deficits found in ADHD often appear.[62] However, it should be pointed out that this area has been widely studied, and many researchers and scientists in the past had oversimplified and overstated the role of this brain area in ADHD.[63] While the prefrontal cortices exert a significant influence over the behaviors that are often deficient in ADHD, researchers have begun to see that this cerebral region is interconnected via neural loops to other areas of the brain, and that these other areas play a significant—though far less understood—role as well.[64]

Irregularities in the cerebellum, for example, are being investigated in ADHD.[65] As neuroimaging techniques improve, researchers will be able to peer more deeply into the brain to solve many of the remaining mysteries. Clearly, many more parts of the brain than previously thought appear to be involved in ADHD,[66] a fact

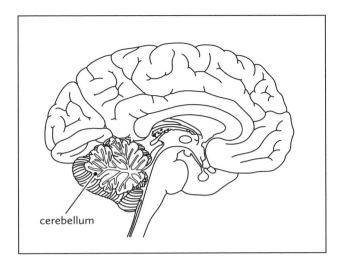

cerebellum

that emphasizes, again, the highly complex nature of the disorder, as well as the interconnected nature of the brain.

The ADHD brain "looks" different than the non-affected brain, and also exhibits dissimilarity in brain wave patterns, a discovery that comes from electroencephalograph (EEG) technologies. The most consistent finding in studies that examined brain wave activity in ADHD individuals is increased theta—or slow-wave—activity, associated with light sleep, and decreased beta activity, associated with wakeful alertness.[67] The ADHD brain, therefore, struggles to stay alert in certain situations. Interestingly, stimulant medications greatly increase the activity of beta waves and decrease theta waves.[68] Data uncovered using fMRI and positron emission tomography (PET) scans show abnormal patterns in the prefrontal cortices and the basal ganglia during certain task and response-inhibition tests that, combined with the EEG data, suggest atypical neural activation patterns in ADHD individuals.[69] The ADHD brain exhibits a variety of structural and functional anomalies that have been shown through numerous studies to ultimately correlate with the behavioral symptoms characteristic of the disorder.

MORE MYSTERIES TO SOLVE

The lay public often misunderstands mental disorders. In the case of ADHD, the symptoms manifest, in general, as behaviors that disrupt school, family, and the workplace. It is almost instinctual for people to use themselves as the standard for judgment when confronted with the atypical behaviors of an ADHD person. This tendency is even more comprehensible when one considers that ADHD symptoms are, by and large, extreme forms of traits that most people exhibit once in a while. The average person, for example, behaves impulsively from time to time, and exhibits poor working memory every so often when forgetting to go back to a task that has been interrupted. Almost all people can think of times of extreme boredom in school when they struggled to pay attention, and most, amid the stress and strain of adult life, struggle on occasion to find keys, wallet, or credit card. People who have these experiences naturally wonder why, if they managed to succeed in school and life, an ADHD person seems to struggle so much. An uninformed person will quickly blame symptoms of ADHD on a deficiency in willpower, on laziness, or on a lack of willingness to accept responsibility. These assumptions, when communicated, can be crushing to an ADHD individual, especially if the messages are experienced from a very young age. ADHD symptoms do often improve with age, but damaged self-esteem may well be a lifelong reality. Educating the public on the neurobiological component of ADHD has the potential to engender greater understanding and compassion and to avoid some of this fallout on self-esteem.

Multiple streams of evidence suggest that ADHD derives from distinct and multiple differences in the brain and *not* from being a choice. The behaviors that define ADHD have been clearly linked, via numerous studies, to deficiencies in the cerebral networks involved in executive functions, impulse control, motor control, attention, arousal, and motivation. Anomalies in size and structure of the brain areas known to be intricately involved in these functions have also been correlated with ADHD. Gene variants that code for dopaminergic and noradrenergic systems carry a strong correlation with the disorder as well, and research has implicated other neurochemicals. Atypical wave and activation patterns have been demonstrated in the ADHD brain. Studies involving brain injuries show that damage to certain parts of the brain can lead to the appearance of ADHD symptoms, providing compelling evidence for the role of the brain and many of its regions in the disorder. Lastly, although the exact mechanisms are not known, medications that improve the symptoms of ADHD are known to act on the regions and systems of the brain that are thought to function atypically in the disorder.

In spite of an enormous body of evidence, however, many unanswered questions remain. Although strong genetic associations and correlations with various regions and networks of the brain have been established, the exact causal mechanisms of the disorder are far from being unlocked, a fact punctuated by the lack of understanding of the different causal pathways involved in the disorder. Not only does research into the neurobiology of ADHD have the potential to lessen the stigma often associated with the disorder, but it also promises to allow earlier diagnosis and provide more effective treatments. As the different causal pathways of ADHD yield more of their secrets, diagnosis might someday be made, or verified, through a blood test, genetic screening, or even cerebral scanning. Treatments have the potential to be more tailored to individual ADHD profiles and thus lead to greater effectiveness and fewer side effects. Whether from injury, early exposure to toxins, or genetic predisposition, ADHD is a disorder that can be understood by examining its signature alterations and variations in the brain. Greater resources to understand its cerebral signature will only help improve the lives of those who suffer with it.

I wish to end this appendix by giving special thanks to Dr. Joel Nigg. His book *What Causes ADHD?* was a primer for my own forays into the neurobiology of ADHD, and I recommend it to anyone who wants to further explore this topic.

NOTES

CHAPTER 1

1. R. Barkley, *Attention-Deficit Hyperactivity Disorder: A Handbook for Diagnosis and Treatment*, 3rd. ed. (New York: Guilford Press, 2006), 226–27.

2. M. Yang, J. Ishii, J. McCracken, J. McGough, S. Loo, S. Nelson, and S. Smalley, "Temperament and Character Profiles and the Dopamine D4 Receptor Gene in ADHD," *American Journal of Psychiatry* 162, no. 5 (2005): 906–14; O. Kebir, K. Tabbane, S. Sengupta, and R. Joober, "Candidate Genes and Neuropsychological Phenotypes in Children with ADHD: Review of Association Studies," *Journal of Psychiatry and Neuroscience* 34, no. 2 (2009): 88–101.

3. W. Simpson and T. Pychyl, "In Search of the Arousal Procrastinator: Investigating the Relation between Procrastination, Arousal-based Personality Traits and Beliefs about Procrastination Motivations," *Personality and Individual Differences* 47, no. 8 (2009): 906–11.

4. J. Biederman, C. Petty, T. Wilens, M. Fraire, C. Purcell, E. Mick, M. Monuteaux, and S. Faraone, "Familial Risk Analyses of Attention Deficit Hyperactivity Disorder and Substance Use Disorder," *American Journal of Psychiatry* 165, no. 1 (2008): 107–15.

5. R. D. Oades, A. G. Sadile, T. Sagvolden, D. Viggiano, A. Zuddas, P. Devoto, H. Aase, E. B. Johansen, L. A. Ruocco, and V. A. Russell, "The Control of Responsiveness in ADHD by Catecholamines: Evidence for Dopaminergic, Noradrenergic and Interactive Roles," *Developmental Science* 8, no. 2 (2005): 123–24.

6. J. Nigg, *What Causes ADHD? Understanding What Goes Wrong and Why* (New York: Guilford Press, 2006), 103.

7. Barkley, *Attention-Deficit Hyperactivity Disorder*, 97.

8. Nigg, *What Causes ADHD?*, 140–41; Barkley, *Attention-Deficit Hyperactivity Disorder*, 144–45.

9. D. Coghill, J. Nigg, A. Rothenberger, E. Sonuga-Barke, and R. Tannock, "Whither Causal Models in the Neuroscience of ADHD?" *Developmental Science* 8, no. 2 (2005): 108–9.

10. Sam Goldstein, CHADD Conference Speech, Atlanta, November 2010.

CHAPTER 2

1. B. S. Bruce, M. Ungar, and D. A. Waschbusch, "Perceptions of Risk among Children with and without Attention Deficit/Hyperactivity Disorder," *International Journal of Injury Control and Safety Promotion* 16, no. 4 (2009): 196–97.

2. Barkley, *Attention-Deficit Hyperactivity Disorder*, 158.

3. Nigg, *What Causes ADHD?*, 54–56.

4. Barkley, *Attention-Deficit Hyperactivity Disorder*, 228–29.

5. John Everingham, personal interview, 2010.

6. A. Anastopoulos, L. Rhoads, and S. Farley, "Counseling and Training Parents," in *Attention-Deficit Hyperactivity Disorder: A Handbook for Diagnosis and Treatment,* 3rd ed., by R. Barkley (New York: Guilford Press, 2006): 453.

7. E. Hallowell and J. Ratey, *Delivered from Distraction* (New York: Random House, 2005), 291.

8. T. Young, "AD/HD through a Parent's Eyes," *The New CHADD Information and Resource Guide to AD/HD* (2006-07): 53.

9. Ibid.

10. D. Amen, *Healing ADD* (New York: Berkley Publishing Group, 2001); E. Berne, *Games People Play* (New York: Random House, 1964).

11. T. Ito, J. Larsen, N. K. Smith, and J. Cacioppo, "Negative Information Weighs More Heavily on the Brain: The Negativity Bias in Evaluative Categorizations," *Journal of Personality and Social Psychology* 75, no. 4 (1998): 887–900.

12. Barkley, *Attention-Deficit Hyperactivity Disorder*, 221–24.

13. M. T. Banich, G. C. Burgess, B. E. Depue, L. Ruzic, L. C. Bidwell, S. Hitt-Laustsen, Y. P. Du, and E. G. Willcutt, "The Neural Basis of Sustained and Transient Attentional Control in Young Adults with ADHD," *Neuropsychologia* 47, no. 14 (2009): 3095–3104.

14. Berne, *Games People Play*.

15. Biederman et al., "Familial Risk Analyses."

16. Nigg, *What Causes ADHD?*, 55–58.

17. S. Smalley, "Reframing ADHD in the Genomic Era," *Psychiatric Times* 25, no. 7 (2008): 74.

18. T. Hartmann, *Attention Deficit Disorder: A Different Perception* (Nevada City, CA: Underwood Books, 1993): 24–25.

19. Ibid., 71–77.

20. R. Bailey, "An Investigation of Personality Types of Adolescents Who Have Been Rated by Classroom Teachers to Exhibit Inattentive and/or Hyperactive-Impulsive Behaviors," (dissertation, University of Arkansas at Little Rock, 1998): 108.

21. S. Brand, R. Dunn, and F. Greb, "Learning Styles of Students with Attention Deficit Hyperactivity Disorder: Who Are They and How Can We Teach Them?" *Clearing House* 75, no. 5 (2002): 268–74.

22. T. Kahler, *The Process Therapy Model* (Little Rock, AR: Kahler Communications, 2008); R. Cordier, A. Bundy, C. Hocking, and S. Einfeld, "A Model for Play-based Intervention for Children with ADHD," *Australian Occupational Therapy Journal* 56, no. 5 (2009): 332–40.

23. Barkley, *Attention-Deficit Hyperactivity Disorder*.

CHAPTER 3

1. Lois Gilman, "Career Advice from Powerful ADHD and LD Executives," *ADDitude* (December/January 2005), see www.additudemag.com/adhd/article/754.html. Marilyn Lewis, "The Upside of ADHD," *MSN Health,* http://health.msn.com/health-topics/adhd/the-upside-of-adhd.

2. A. Taylor, and F. Kuo, "Children with Attention Deficits Concentrate Better after Walk in the Park," *Journal of Attention Disorder* 10 (2008): 1077.

3. Hartmann, *Attention Deficit Disorder*.

4. J. M. Fuster, *The Prefrontal Cortex: Anatomy, Physiology and Neuropsychology of the Prefrontal Lobe*, 3rd ed. (New York: Raven Press, 1997).

5. Nigg, *What Causes ADHD?*, 122–26.

6. Ibid., 114–15.

7. Amen, *Healing ADD*, 178–88.

8. A. Cowan, L. David, and J. Seinfeld, *Seinfeld*, "The Opposite," episode 86, season 5. First Aired: Thursday, May 9, 1994.

9. T. D. Vloet, K. Konrad, B. Herpertz-Dahlmann, G. G. Polier, and T. Gunther, "Impact of Anxiety Disorders on Attentional Functions in Children with ADHD," *Journal of Affective Disorders* 124, no. 3 (2010): 283–90.

10. I. Singh, T. Kendall, C. Taylor, A. Mears, C. Hollis, M. Batty, and S. Keenan, "Experience of ADHD and Stimulant Medication:

A Qualitative Study for the NICE Guidelines: Young People's Experience of ADHD and Stimulant Medication," *Child and Adolescent Mental Health* 15, no. 4 (2010): 186–92.

CHAPTER 4

1. Amen, *Healing ADD*, 178–88.
2. G. Bodenmann, N. Meuwly, T. N. Bradbury, S. Gmelch, and T. Ledermann, "Stress, Anger, and Verbal Aggression in Intimate Relationships: Moderating Effects of Individual and Dyadic Coping," *Journal of Social and Personal Relationships* 27, no. 3 (2010): 408–24.
3. D. Goleman, *Emotional Intelligence* (New York: Bantam Books, 1995), 16.
4. "Gratitude Is Good Medicine for Organ Recipients," *Science Daily*, August 2007. Available at www.sciencedaily.com/releases/2007 /08/070815135030.htm.
5. Ibid.

CHAPTER 5

1. J. Nigg, L. Blaskey, C. Huang-Pollock, S. Hinshaw, O. P. John, E. Willcutt, and B. Pennington, "Big Five Dimensions and ADHD Symptoms: Links between Personality Traits and Clinical Symptoms," *Journal of Personality and Social Psychology* 83, no. 2 (2002): 451–69; A. Robin, A. Tzelepis, and M. Bedway, "A Cluster Analysis of Personality Style in Adults with ADHD," *Journal of Attention Disorders* 12 (2008): 254–63; Bailey, "An Investigation of Personality Types," 108.
2. P. Roussos, S. G. Giakoumaki, and P. Bitsios, "Cognitive and Emotional Processing in High Novelty Seeking Associated with the L-DRD4 Genotype," *Neuropsychologia* 47, no. 7 (2009): 1654–59; Barkley, *Attention-Deficit Hyperactivity Disorder*.
3. K. Langley, L. Marshall, M. van den Bree, H. Thomas, M. Owen, M. O'Donovan, and A. Thapar, "Association of the Dopamine D4 Receptor Gene 7-Repeat Allele with Neuropsychological Test Performance of Children with ADHD," *American Journal of Psychiatry* 161, no. 1 (2004): 133–38; Barkley, *Attention-Deficit Hyperactivity Disorder*.
4. Hartmann, *Attention Deficit Disorder*.
5. M. Edmundson, "Playing the Fool," *New York Times* (April 2000).
6. J. Sobran, "Lear's Fool," *The Real News of the Month*, August 18,

2005. Griffen Internet Syndicate. Available at www.sobran.com /columns/2005/050818.shtml.

7. S. F. Dingfelder, "The Formula for Funny," *Monitor on Psychology* 37, no. 6 (2006): 54.

8. Anthony Vicich, personal interview, 2010.

9. G. Dean, *Step by Step to Standup Comedy* (Portsmouth, NH: Heineman, 2000); Vicich, personal interview.

10. Dean, *Step by Step to Standup Comedy*, 3.

11. J. Carter, *Stand-up Comedy: The Book* (New York: Bantam Doubleday Bell, 1989).

12. Vicich, personal interview.

13. Everingham, personal interview.

14. Kahler, *The Process Therapy Model*; M. Gilbert, *Communicating Effectively: Tools for Educational Leaders* (Lanham, MD: Scarecrow Education, 2004); Cordier et al., "A Model for Play-based Intervention."

15. M. Sorensen, "Humor as a Serious Strategy of Nonviolent Resistance to Oppression," *Peace and Change* 33, no. 2 (2008): 167–90.

16. M. J. Elias and L. Erickson, "The Therapeutic Power of Humor," *Saturday Evening Post* 272, no. 2 (2000).

17. B. Druss and R. Rosenheck, "Depressed and/or SA Patients Use More Health Care Than General Population," *DATA: The Brown University Digest of Addiction Theory and Application* 18, no. 6 (1999): 3–4.

18. "Hearty Humor," *Harvard Men's Health Watch* 13 no. 9 (2009): 7.

19. M. Stuber, S. Hilber, L. Mintzer, M. Castaneda, D. Glover, and L. Zeltzer, "Laughter, Humor and Pain Perception in Children: A Pilot Study," *Evidence-Based Complementary and Alternative Medicine (eCAM)* 6, no. 2 (2009): 271–76.

CHAPTER 6

1. Kahler, *The Process Therapy Model*; Cordier et al., "A Model for Play-based Intervention."

2. Amen, *Healing ADD*.

3. E. Willcut, A. Doyle, J. Nigg, S. Faraone, and B. Pennington, "Validity of the Executive Function Theory of Attention Deficit/ Hyperactivity Disorder: A Meta-Analytic Review," *Biological Psychiatry* 57 (2005): 1336–46.

4. Barkley, *Attention-Deficit Hyperactivity Disorder*.

5. Ibid; G. Tripp and J. Wickens, "Neurobiology of ADHD," *Neuropharmacology* 57, no. 7/8 (2010): 579–89.

6. N. M. Evangelista, J. Owens, C. M. Golden, and W. Pelham Jr., "The Positive Illusory Bias: Do Inflated Self-Perceptions in Children with ADHD Generalize to Perceptions of Others?" *Journal of Abnormal Child Psychology* 36, no. 5 (2008): 779–91.

7. Kahler, *The Process Therapy Model.*

8. Ibid.; Gilbert, *Communicating Effectively*; Cordier et al., "A Model for Play-Based Intervention."

9. M. Gilbert, "Process Communication Model: Seven-Day Seminar," Class Lecture and Discussion, Central Michigan University, 2009.

10. Vicich, personal interview.

11. http://misterguch.brinkster.net/chemfiestanew.html.

12. Barkley, *Attention-Deficit Hyperactivity Disorder*, 157.

13. P. Corkum, H. Moldofsky, S. Hogg-Johnson, T. Humphries, and R. Tannock, "Sleep Problems in Children with Attention Deficit/Hyperactivity Disorder: Impact of Subtype, Comorbidity, and Stimulant Medication," *Journal of the American Academy of Child and Adolescent Psychiatry* 38 (1999): 1285–93.

14. J. Meaux, A. Green, and L. Broussard, "ADHD in the College Student: A Block in the Road," *Journal of Psychiatric and Mental Health Nursing* 16, no. 3 (2009): 248–56.

CHAPTER 7

1. Barkley, *Attention-Deficit Hyperactivity Disorder.*

2. Hartmann, *Attention Deficit Disorder*, 24–26.

3. R. Merrill, J. Lyon, R. Baker, and L. Gren, "Attention Deficit Hyperactivity Disorder and Increased Risk of Injury," *Advances in Medical Sciences* 54, no. 1 (2009): 20–26.

4. Hallowell and Ratey, *Delivered from Distraction*, 219–20.

5. Kahler, *The Process Therapy Model.*

6. C. E. Cunningham, *Attention Deficit Hyperactivity Disorder: A Handbook for Diagnosis and Treatment* (New York: Guilford Press, 2006).

7. Cunningham, *Attention Deficit Hyperactivity Disorder*; M. Leary and R. Miller, *Social Psychology and Dysfunctional Behavior* (New York: Springer-Verlag, 1986).

8. K. MacKenzie, *Introduction to Time Limited Group Psychotherapy* (Washington, DC: American Psychiatric Press, 1990).

9. T. Hirvikoski, E. Waaler, J. Alfredsson, C. Pihlgren, A. Holmström, A. Johnson, J. Rück, C. Wiwe, P. Bothén, and A. L. Nordström, "Reduced ADHD Symptoms in Adults with ADHD after Structured Skills Training Group: Results from a Randomized Controlled Trial," *Behaviour Research and Therapy* 49, no. 3 (2011).

10. MacKenzie, *Introduction to Time Limited Group Psychotherapy*.

11. P. Plummer and G. Stoner, "The Relative Effects of Classwide Peer Tutoring and Peer Coaching on Positive Social Behaviors of Children with ADHD," *Journal of Attention Disorders* 9, no. 1 (2005): 290–300; G. DuPaul and T. Eckert, "The Effects of Social Skills Curricula: Now You See Them, Now You Don't," *School Psychology Quarterly* 9 (1994): 112–32; F. Gresham, "Teaching Social Skills to High-Risk Children and Youth: Preventative and Remedial Strategies," in *Interventions for Academic and Behavioral Problems II: Preventative and Remedial Approaches*, ed. M. Shinn (Bethesda, MD: National Association of School Psychologists, 2002), 403–32; B. Hoza, S. Mrug, W. Peklham, A. Greiner, and E. Gnagy, "A Friendship Intervention for Children with Attention Deficit/Hyperactivity Disorder: Preliminary Findings," *Journal of Attention Disorders* 6 (2003): 86–98; S. Mrug, B. Hoza, and A. Gerdes, "Children with Attention Deficit/Hyperactivity Disorder: Peer Relationships and Peer-Oriented Interventions," in "The Role of Friendship in Psychological Adjustment," special issue, *New Directions for Child and Adolescent Development* 91 (2001): 51–78.

12. Cordier et al., "A Model for Play-based Intervention."

13. C. Bagwell, B. Molina, W. E. Pelham, and B. Hoza, "Attention-Deficit Hyperactivity Disorder and Problems in Peer Relations: Predictions from Childhood to Adolescence," *Journal of the American Academy of Child and Adolescent Psychiatry* 40, no. 11 (2001): 1285–92; B. Hoza, S. Mrug, A. Gerdes, S. P. Hinshaw, W. Bukowski, J. A. Gold, H. Kraerner, W. Pelham Jr., T. Wigal, and E. L. Arnold, "What Aspects of Peer Relationships Are Impaired in Children with Attention-Deficit/Hyperactivity Disorder?" *Journal of Consulting and Clinical Psychology* 73, no. 3 (2005): 411–23.

14. Cordier et al., "A Model for Play-based Intervention."

15. K. Kolbe, *Pure Instinct: The M.O. of High Performance People and Teams* (Phoenix AZ: Monumentis Press, 2004), 13.

APPENDIX

1. Nigg, *What Causes ADHD?*, 274–75.

2. Centers for Disease Control, "Mental Health in the United States: Prevalence of Diagnosis and Medication Treatment for Attention-Deficit/Hyperactivity Disorder—United States, 2003," *Morbidity and Morality Weekly Report* 54, no. 34 (2005): 842–47. Available at www.cdc.gov/mmwr/preview/mmwrhtml/mm5434a2.htm.

3. A. Robin, personal interview, July 25, 2011.

4. C. Zeigler, "Executive Function: What Is It Anyway?" Available at www.chrisdendy.com/executive.htm.

5. Nigg, *What Causes ADHD?*, 74.

6. Barkley, *Attention-Deficit Hyperactivity Disorder*, 226.

7. Nigg, *What Causes ADHD?*, 196; N. Williams, I. Zaharieva, A. Martin, K. Langley, K. Mantripragada, R. Fossdal, H. Stefansson, K. Stefansson, P. Magnusson, O. Gudmundsson, O. Gustafsson, P. Holmans, M. Owen, M. O'Donovan, and A. Thapar, "Rare Chromosomal Deletions and Duplications in Attention-Deficit Hyperactivity Disorder: A Genome-Wide Analysis," *Lancet* 376, no. 9750 (2010): 1401–08.

8. Nigg, *What Causes ADHD?*

9. N. Rommelse, M. Altink, J. Oosterlaan, C. Buschgens, J. Buitelaar, L. De Sonneville, and J. Sergeant, "Motor Control in Children with ADHD and Non-affected Siblings: Deficits Most Pronounced Using the Left Hand," *Journal of Child Psychology and Psychiatry* 48, no. 11 (2007): 1071–79; Nigg, *What Causes ADHD?*, 162.

10. S. Gau and S. Chi-Yung, "Executive Functions as Endophenotypes in ADHD: Evidence from the Cambridge Neuropsychological Test Battery (CANTAB)," *Journal of Child Psychology and Psychiatry* 51, no. 7 (2010): 838–49.

11. S. Durston, P. Hulshoff, H. Schnack, J. Buitelaar, M. Steenhuis, R. Minderaa, R. Kahn, and H. van Engeland, "Magnetic Resonance Imaging of Boys with Attention Deficit Disorder and Their Unaffected Siblings," *Journal of the American Academy of Child and Adolescent Psychiatry* 43, no. 3 (2004): 332–40.

12. S. Loo, E. Rich, J. Ishii, J. McGough, J. McCracken, S. Nelson, and S. Smalley, "Cognitive Functioning in Affected Sibling Pairs with ADHD: Familial Clustering and Dopamine Genes," *Journal of Child Psychology and Psychiatry* 49, no. 9 (2008): 950–57; L. Bidwell, E. Willcutt, M. McQueen, J. DeFries, R. Olson, S. Smith, and B. Pennington, "A Family-Based Association Study of DRD4, DAT1, and 5HTT and

Continuous Traits of Attention-Deficit Hyperactivity Disorder," *Behavior Genetics* 41, no. 1 (2011): 165–74.

13. A. C. Bédard, K. Schulz, E. Cook, J. Fan, S. Clerkin, I. Ivanov, J. Halperin, and J. Newcorn, "Dopamine Transporter Gene Variation Modulates Activation of Striatum in Youth with ADHD," *NeuroImage* 53, no. 3 (2010): 935–42; Nigg, *What Causes ADHD?*; S. Loo, E. Specter, A. Smolen, C. Hopfer, P. Teale, and M. Reite, "Functional Effects of the DAT1 Polymorphism on EEG Measures in ADHD," *Journal of the American Academy of Child and Adolescent Psychiatry* 42 (2003): 986–93.

14. Bidwell et al., "A Family-based Association Study."

15. J. Biederman, S. Faraone, E. Mick, T. Spencer, T. Wilens, K. Kiely, J. Guite, J. S. Ablon, E. Reed, and R. Warburton, "High Risk for Attention Deficit Hyperactivity Disorder among Children of Parents with Childhood Onset of the Disorder: A Pilot Study," *American Journal of Psychiatry* 152, no. 3 (1995): 431–35.

16. Barkley, *Attention-Deficit Hyperactivity Disorder*, 226; Nigg, *What Causes ADHD?*, 194.

17. Williams et al., "Rare Chromosomal Deletions and Duplications."

18. Nigg, *What Causes ADHD?*, 117–18.

19. P. Howard, *The Owner's Manual for the Brain* (Austin, TX: Bard Press, 2007).

20. R. Suri, "TD Models of Predictive Responses in Dopamine Neurons," *Neural Networks* 15 (2002): 523–33; Fuster, *The Prefrontal Cortex*.

21. R. A. Ruden, *The Craving Brain*, 2nd ed. (New York: Harper Collins, 1997).

22. Ibid.

23. Suri, "TD Models of Predictive Responses."

24. G. Tripp and J. Wickens, "Neurobiology of ADHD," *Neuropharmacology* 57, no. 7/8 (2009): 579–89.

25. Nigg, *What Causes ADHD?*, 207.

26. Ibid., 149.

27. Tripp and Wickens, "Neurobiology of ADHD."

28. Nigg, *What Causes ADHD?*, 149–50.

29. Tripp and Wickens, "Neurobiology of ADHD."

30. Nigg, *What Causes ADHD?*, 56–57.

31. Ibid., 58–59; Barkley, *Attention-Deficit Hyperactivity Disorder*, 220–23.

32. Nigg, *What Causes ADHD?*, 61.

33. F. Castellanos, J. Giedd, and W. Marsh, "Quantitative Brain Magnetic Resonance Imaging in ADHD," *Archives of General Psychiatry* 53 (1996): 607–16; M. Solanto, "Dopamine Dysfunction in AD/HD: Integrating Clinical and Basic Neuroscience Research," *Behavioural Brain Research* 130 (2002): 65–71.

34. P. Taepavarapruk, S. Floresco, and A. Phillips, "Hyperlocomotion and Increased Dopamine Efflux in the Nucleus Accumbens Evoked by Electrical Stimulation of the Ventral Subiculum: Role of Ionotropic Glutamate and Dopamine D1 Receptors," *Psychopharmacology* 151 (2000): 242–51.

35. C. Luhmann, "Temporal Decision-Making: Insights from Cognitive Neuroscience," *Frontiers in Behavioral Neuroscience* 3, no. 39 (October 23, 2009).

36. Nigg, *What Causes ADHD?*, 205.

37. Ibid.; J. M. Swanson, P. Floodman, J. Kennedy, M. Spence, R. Moyzis, S. Schuck, M. Murias, J. Moriarity, C. Barr, M. Smith, and M. Posner, "Dopamine Genes and ADHD," *Neuroscience and Biobehavioral Reviews* 24, no. 1 (2000): 21–25.

38. N. Volkow, G. Wang, J. Fowler, J. Logan, D. Franceschi, and L. Maynard. "Relationship between Blockade of Dopamine Transporters by Oral Methylphenidate and the Increases in Extracellular Dopamine: Therapeutic Implications," *Synapse* 43 (2002): 181–87; D. Connor, "Stimulants," in *Attention-Deficit Hyperactivity Disorder: A Handbook for Diagnosis and Treatment,* 3rd ed., by R. Barkley (New York: Guilford Press, 2006), 608–647.

39. Connor, "Stimulants."

40. Nigg, *What Causes ADHD?*, 159–60.

41. Connor, "Stimulants."

42. T. Spencer, "Antidepressant and Specific Norepinephrine Reuptake Inhibitor Treatment," in *Attention-Deficit Hyperactivity Disorder: A Handbook for Diagnosis and Treatment,* 3rd ed., by R. Barkley (New York: Guilford Press, 2006), 653; S. Quartz and R. Sejnowski, *Liars, Lovers, and Heroes: What the New Brain Science Reveals about How We Become Who We Are* (New York: Quill/Harper Collins, 2002), 96; E. Tzavara, D. Li, L. Moutsimilli, T. Bisogno, V. Marzo, L. Phebus, G. Nomikos, and B. Giros, "Endocannabinoids Activate Transient Receptor Potential Vanilloid 1 Receptors to Reduce Hyperdopaminergia-Related Hyperactivity: Therapeutic Implications," *Biological Psychiatry*

59, no. 6 (2006): 508–15.

43. Howard, *The Owner's Manual for the Brain*.

44. Ibid., 56.

45. Nigg, *What Causes ADHD?*, 60–61.

46. Barkley, *Attention-Deficit Hyperactivity Disorder*; Nigg, *What Causes ADHD?*

47. Spencer, "Antidepressant and Specific," 653.

48. D. Connor, K. Fletcher, and J. Swanson, "A Meta-Analysis of Clonidine for Symptoms of Attention-Deficit Hyperactivity Disorder," *Journal of the American Academy of Child and Adolescent Psychiatry* 38 (1999): 826–34; Spencer, "Antidepressant and Specific."

49. K. Boong-Nyun, K. Jae-Won, K. Hyejin, C. Soo-Churl, S. Min-Sup, Y. Hee-Jeong, H. Soon-Beom, and L. Dong Soo, "Regional Differences in Cerebral Perfusion Associated with the α-2A-Adrenergic Receptor Genotypes in Attention Deficit Hyperactivity Disorder," *Journal of Psychiatry and Neuroscience* 35, no. 5 (2010): 330–36.

50. Howard, *The Owner's Manual for the Brain*, 57; Nigg, *What Causes ADHD?*, 60.

51. Nigg, *What Causes ADHD?*, 60–61.

52. M. Hoskison, A. Moore, B. Hu, S. Orsi, N. Kobori, and P. Dash, "Persistent Working Memory Dysfunction Following Traumatic Brain Injury: Evidence for a Time-Dependent Mechanism," *Neuroscience* 159, no. 2 (2009): 483–91.

53. Nigg, *What Causes ADHD?*

54. Ibid; L. Seidman, E. Valera, and N. Makris, "Structural Brain Imaging of Attention Deficit/Hyperactivity Disorder," *Biological Psychiatry* 57 (2005): 1263–72.

55. Nigg, *What Causes ADHD?*

56. K. Narr, R. Woods, J. Lin, J. Kim, O. Phillips, M. Del'Homme, R. Caplan, A. Toga, J. McCracken, and J. Levitt, "Widespread Cortical Thinning Is a Robust Anatomical Marker for Attention-Deficit/Hyperactivity Disorder," *Journal of the American Academy of Child and Adolescent Psychiatry* 48 (2009): 1014–22.

57. I. Ellison-Wright, Z. Ellison-Wright, and E. Bullmore, "Structural Brain Change in Attention Deficit Hyperactivity Disorder Identified by Meta-Analysis," *BMC Psychiatry* 8 (2008): 1–8; Nigg, *What Causes ADHD?*; X. Cao, Q. Cao, X. Long, L. Sun, M. Sui, C. Zhu, X. Zuo, Y. Zang, and Y. Wang, "Abnormal Resting-State Functional

Connectivity Patterns of the Putamen in Medication-Naïve Children with Attention Deficit Hyperactivity Disorder," *Brain Research* 1303 (2009): 195–206.

58. Ellison-Wright et al., "Structural Brain Change."

59. A. Qiu, D. Crocetti, M. Adler, E. M. Mahone, M. Denckla, M. Miller, and S. Mostofsky, "Basal Ganglia Volume and Shape in Children With Attention Deficit Hyperactivity Disorder," *American Journal of Psychiatry* 166, no. 1 (2009): 74–82.

60. Qiu et al., "Basal Ganglia Volume"; S. Mostofsky, K. Cooper, W. Kates, M. Denckla, and W. Kaufmann, "Smaller Prefrontal and Premotor Volumes in Boys with ADHD," *Biological Psychiatry* 52 (2002): 785–94.

61. Barkley, *Attention-Deficit Hyperactivity Disorder*.

62. Fuster, *The Prefrontal Cortex*; Nigg, *What Causes ADHD?*; Hoskison et al., "Persistent Working Memory Dysfunction."

63. Nigg, *What Causes ADHD?*, 105–9.

64. Nigg, *What Causes ADHD?*; A. Arnsten, "Toward a New Understanding of Attention-Deficit Hyperactivity Disorder Pathophysiology: An Important Role for Prefrontal Cortex Dysfunction," *CNS Drugs* 23, Suppl. 1 (2009): 33–41.

65. S. Carmona, O. Vilarroya, A. Bielsa, V. Trèmols, J. Soliva, M. Rovira, J. Tomàs, C. Raheb, J. Gispert, S. Batlle, and A. Bulbena, "Global and Regional Gray Matter Reductions in ADHD: A Voxelbased Morphometric Study," *Neuroscience Letters* 389, no. 2 (2005): 88–93; Nigg, *What Causes ADHD?*; S. Durston, and K. Konrad, "Integrating Genetic, Psychopharmacological and Neuroimaging Studies: A Converging Methods Approach to Understanding the Neurobiology of ADHD," *Developmental Review* 27, no. 3 (2007): 374–95.

66. Nigg, *What Causes ADHD?*

67. Barkley, *Attention-Deficit Hyperactivity Disorder*; Howard, *The Owner's Manual for the Brain*.

68. Barkley, *Attention-Deficit Hyperactivity Disorder*.

69. Nigg, *What Causes ADHD?*

ABOUT THE AUTHOR

Kevin Roberts has a master's degree in ADHD Studies from Antioch University. His background is in education, and for more than thirteen years he has been a life coach, helping folks dealing with ADHD and other learning differences succeed in school and life. A stand-up comedian, Roberts believes teaching people with ADHD how to find the fun in life provides a powerful key to success. As a nationally recognized speaker, Roberts has trained therapists, physicians, nurses, teachers, parents, and school administrators about ADHD as well as the perils of the Internet, smart phones, and video games. His first book, *Cyber Junkie: Escape the Gaming and Internet Trap,* was published by Hazelden in 2010.

Roberts is the cofounder, board member, and curriculum developer of The EmpowerADD Project, a nonprofit organization that helps ADHD young adults discover lives of successful purpose. You can find more information at www.empoweradd.org. Roberts is also a member of the Honorable Order of Kentucky Colonels.

Hazelden, a national nonprofit organization founded in 1949, helps people reclaim their lives from the disease of addiction. Built on decades of knowledge and experience, Hazelden offers a comprehensive approach to addiction that addresses the full range of patient, family, and professional needs, including treatment and continuing care for youth and adults, research, higher learning, public education and advocacy, and publishing.

A life of recovery is lived "one day at a time." Hazelden publications, both educational and inspirational, support and strengthen lifelong recovery. In 1954, Hazelden published *Twenty-Four Hours a Day*, the first daily meditation book for recovering alcoholics, and Hazelden continues to publish works to inspire and guide individuals in treatment and recovery, and their loved ones. Professionals who work to prevent and treat addiction also turn to Hazelden for evidence-based curricula, informational materials, and videos for use in schools, treatment programs, and correctional programs.

Through published works, Hazelden extends the reach of hope, encouragement, help, and support to individuals, families, and communities affected by addiction and related issues.

For questions about Hazelden publications,
please call **800-328-9000**
or visit us online at **hazelden.org/bookstore**.